contents

THE SUNDAY TIM

..ping

⊃ur

Staff

Patrick Forsyth

△ KOGAN PAGE | *CREATING SUCCESS*

First published in 2001

Kogan Page Limited
120 Pentonville Road
London N1 9JN

The views expressed in this book are those of the author, and are not necessarily the same as those of Times Newspapers Ltd.

British Library Cataloguing in Publication Data

A CIP record for this book is available from the British Library.

ISBN 0 7494 3525 9

Typeset by Jean Cussons Typesetting, Diss, Norfolk
Printed and bound in Great Britain by Clays Ltd, St Ives plc

preface

Sending men into war without training is like abandoning them.

Confucius

As the 21st century gets under way, the job of management is a challenging business. The job exists unequivocally to achieve results. Whatever results a particular functional role may dictate – revenue, productivity, cost reduction and so on – the pressures to achieve are often relentless. The busy manager may feel so beset with problems that it is difficult to call them challenges and to view them positively.

Certainly pressures have increased in recent years. There never seems to be enough time or resources. There always seems to be too much administration, paperwork and general indecision and hassle. Probably no one works in a perfect environment, or ever will, but any manager with a team of other people to manage has a significant antidote to all this — his or her staff.

Results cannot usually be achieved by any single manager just 'doing it all themselves'. All the good things we want as managers: efficiency, effectiveness, productivity, creativity and ultimately results, are best achieved by the whole team working effectively, both as a team and as individuals. Thus everyone needs to be good at his or her own job. This of course means that they must be good at the individual tasks their job entails.

These may be anything from conducting persuasive meetings with customers to interviewing job applicants or progressing complex projects, depending on the role of the job. Proficiency at the processes it involves along the way, eg making decisions, report writing or time management, is also necessary.

And nobody's perfect.

Development – and training, its more formal partner – is essential if staff performance is to be maximised. Other things matter too, of course; motivation for example, which goes hand in hand with development in some ways (more of this later). But development has a particular and a significant role to play. This is easy to say, and sounds essentially common sense – which it surely is. As the old saying has it: 'If you think training is expensive, try ignorance.' But the logic of its necessity does not automatically mean development will just happen. Nor does it make doing it easy.

There are all too many potential difficulties:

- lack of time;
- inadequate resources;
- under-funded training budgets;
- conflicting priorities;
- lack of clarity about what should be done;
- failure to identify, or accept, the need;
- shortfall in training skill or experience.

Any, or all, of the above (and more) can conspire to ensure that training and development do not occur. Or that they are done too little, too late or otherwise fudged. Despite this, it may be worth noting – in part from a competitive viewpoint – that the time and money being spent on training and development are in fact increasing. At the time of writing, for example, the Institute of Management's survey, 'Achieving Management Excellence', has just shown this. It also shows that attitudes to development as a necessary and desirable activity were more positive than in the past (the survey is available from the UK Institute of Management, tel: 01536 204222).

If proper staff development makes a difference (and this book certainly takes the view that it does) then the job of doing it and making it work must be tackled. This book sets out to establish the need, and to show just what you can gain by good development policies and action. It also sets out something about the detail that makes choice of development methods and activities, and their ongoing implementation, successful.

Development may occur for many reasons, for example:

▓ as part of an individual's long-term career growth;
▓ to add or enhance skills needed in the short term;
▓ being necessary to fill a gap in past performance;
▓ to move ahead or keep up with change.

Whatever the reason for it, and whatever its purpose, its execution must be approached in an appropriate way. This is, not least, because inappropriate action may do more harm than good and, at worst, it may fail to improve performance and act to demotivate staff in the process.

Change alone (and the pace of change seems to accelerate as you watch) provides ample reason to take an active view of the development process. The recent history of IT (information technology) is a good example. Once upon a time, when writing a book like this I would have drafted it in longhand, a secretary would have typed it and the process would have proceeded from there. Now I type it, but I have had to learn to type and to operate the word processor and the electronic mail that keeps me in touch with the publisher during the process. And such systems do not stand still. The learning process continues. Much of what is going on in organisations is inherently much more complex than this – and all the skills that need deploying must keep pace.

So, you may say, I agree with all this – but that is what

training departments are for, I have enough to do – let them provide what is needed. Perhaps they can; certainly in an organisation of any size such a department will have a role to play.

But the responsibility to develop people resides *with the individual manager*. It is a responsibility that goes with the territory. If you have people reporting to you then you have to act to ensure that development takes place to establish, certainly to maintain, their ability to do a good job now and in the future. That need not mean the manager must personally provide all the development that takes place, but it is likely to mean he or she initiates most of it. This book is intended to provide some guidelines for managers wanting to exercise that responsibility.

The results that can be achieved make the time and effort it takes (for both management and staff) worthwhile. There will always be apparently good reasons not to act, or to delay. Just one is the old chestnut: 'What a waste if I develop my staff and then they leave.' To which the only logical response is: 'What if you *don't* develop them – and they stay?'

Good people and good performance – and hence good development – are fundamental to success in a fast-changing and competitive world. Your organisation's success – and that of you and your team – may depend, in part, on getting this right.

Patrick Forsyth, 2001

Touchstone Training & Consultancy
28 Saltcote Maltings
Heybridge
Maldon
Essex CM9 4QP

attitudes to development

The prime asset of any manager, of any organisation for that matter, is people. The manager has many responsibilities, but two rank especially high: those of ensuring people are *able* to deliver, and undertake whatever is necessary to meet their objectives, and ensuring people *want* to produce the desired performance.

Development is crucial to the first, motivation to the second and, as we will see, these two must go hand in hand.

Before continuing, consider the scope of development. Essentially it can do three things:

1. impart knowledge;
2. develop skills;
3. change attitudes.

Sometimes it must do all three together, though the timescales may vary and, as a general rule, it takes longer to change attitudes – especially long-held ones – than to get new facts across. The purposes of any sort of development may vary widely. It may be to:

- extend knowledge;
- introduce new skills, adding to the range available in an individual or a group;
- fine-tune existing skills, producing a greater level of performance in the future;
- prompt fresh thinking and ideas, and play a part in evolving new ways of doing things.

It may be intended to have an immediate effect or initiate a radical change longer term. Its relationship with targets and the results people may be charged with achieving may be close, or it may be that a more general effect is intended. In addition, just to make the span of influence clear, it may be linked to a host of other factors such as:

- changing organisation structure;
- decentralisation or links around an organisation with multiple locations;
- technological change;
- change in business practice, policy or culture;
- market and competitive change.

Development should always make a difference; a positive difference that helps make an organisation stronger, more effective and better able to cope with the challenging environment in which it doubtless must exist. Again the potential results of training are many, including:

- extended staff retention;
- increased job flexibility;
- competitive advantage;
- faster response to events;
- improved motivation (and lower incidence of absence and accidents).

So, development is necessary. Its execution is worthwhile and, like any management task, it must be done in a way that maximises the results from the time and effort involved. It does not just happen, of course, it does take time – though one of the objectives of this book is to show that a great deal can be done with modest time and money.

Right, so accepting that training and development are 'good things', how do people view them?

staff attitudes

In many organisations there is a general sense of approval about development. How much training is done certainly varies over time. In any period of recession, for instance, whether it affects the general economy or is something that affects a particular industry, training (like promotion) is some-thing that appears easy to cut back on short term. Often this is what happens. One senior manager (Jeremy Thorn) is quoted as saying:

> Regardless of what you manage, wherever there are goals to be achieved by organising and directing the resources and efforts of others, your watchword must be professionalism. This requires skill, experience and training, for effective managers are not born, they need to be trained and developed. This investment in training is like any other: if it is made wisely it will pay rich dividends; and it should never stop, for no one can know it all.

Fair comment. It defines training as an investment and makes the point that it is a continuous process. If this is the feeling throughout an organisation, and if it is backed by appropriate resources, including a suitable budget, then it should make it easier to ensure that the development activity that follows makes a difference.

In this context, how is an individual likely to feel? What, in fact, do members of your staff, or team, think? First, consider how they are likely to view their job and the way it is supervised. To do so it is worth a brief digression regarding motivation.

motivation

A picture of how motivation works – why people take the attitude they do to work, job and employer – can draw on a plethora of theories. Just two factors will provide a workable framework, however, essentially envisaging a balance of changing positive and negative influences, the net effect of which produces the individual's prevailing motivational state. Each heading may encompass many different factors and the way influence can be brought to bear is largely in the details. This way of looking at motivation draws on the fundamentals from Herzberg's theory of dissatisfiers (or hygiene factors), and satisfiers (or motivators).

The following list – shown with examples of how each factor can tie in with training and development – will act to summarise. Let's consider positive areas first.

the satisfiers

Key influences on creating positive feelings are:

▨ *Achievement:* people like to achieve, and therefore want and favour anything that will help them do so. Development (well, good development) is likely to be seen as helpful, something that will make achievement more likely.

▨ *Recognition:* achievement alone is one thing; people like to *know* they have achieved something – and they like feedback that tells them so. Development may be seen as stemming from such feedback: they do well and this puts them in line to do more and development makes this possible.

▓ *The work itself:* people prefer, not unnaturally, to enjoy or at least get some satisfaction from work. Development can make work easier, take someone into new areas and avoid the hassle of struggling while ill-equipped in some way.

▓ *Responsibility:* most people want this (indeed in most organisations getting it is, in part, a recognition of achievement); again this makes developmental help attractive.

▓ *Advancement:* this is doing more, different and maybe more interesting things (and ultimately involves the formal change of promotion). Most people would take the view that development can play a part in making this possible.

▓ *Growth:* this implies more than promotion, moving on (for example to a new part of the organisation or out beyond into another); here too this is only likely to be possible if people have suitable capabilities.

the dissatisfiers

Key factors that can create negative feelings and dilute any overall positive view are:

▓ *Company policy and administrative processes:* anything nonsensical or bureaucratic rankles; likewise policy that precludes development or makes it difficult or minimal.

▓ *Supervision:* if you manage people, this is you; and people will expect you to be sympathetic – indeed actively helpful – to their enjoyment of and progress in their job; so again there are clear development implications.

■ *Working conditions:* this can involve so much, and anything that makes doing the job more difficult than it should be (or is perceived as doing so) can dilute motivation. Lack of training can easily fall into this category.

■ *Salary and rewards:* if the package is not 'right' demotivation can quickly result. These days training may be seen (virtually) as part of the package.

■ *Relationship with peers:* various factors might come under this heading; for example perceived unfairness when some are trained and some are not may cause problems.

■ *Personal life (and the impact of work on it):* less direct influences here perhaps; but long training away from home might be a problem.

■ *Status:* less tangible in nature (as with security, below) but no less important; it affects matters in many ways. Training and development might link to this in various ways: doing training being seen as bestowing status or, in the wrong environment, not.

■ *Security:* not just job security, but the security of clear objectives and knowing what to do and how to do it; the latter has a clear link with development.

Some of these may be relevant in your organisation and you may be able to add others to the list. Some you may be able to control directly, others you may be able to influence. For example, you may not have responsibility for an internal staff newsletter, but you may be able to contribute articles or features to it if doing so would be useful to you and your people.

Of course there is more to motivation than this. For more about the whole area see my book *How to Motivate People* (also in the Kogan Page/Sunday Times 'Creating Success' series).

management implications

Although there can be exceptions (being sent on a course because of some fault or failure, perhaps), your staff are certainly likely to regard training and development as desirable, indeed even as essential. One thing that always reminds me of this is the many surveys I have seen, asking people to list in order of desirability the characteristics that they would like to have in the 'perfect' manager. Many factors are always listed. That managers should be fair, good listeners, skilled at their own job, decisive and more.

One factor, however, consistently comes at or near the top of such a list. People say: 'I want to work with a manager from whom I learn.' Further questioning reveals that this is seen in two ways. First, learning direct from their contact with the manager; second, learning from the development that a manager organises for them (for example, arranging attendance on a course).

The lesson could not be clearer. Development may be good – necessary – for all sorts of reasons, but always because people want and enjoy it. The manager who ignores the development of his or her staff, or is seen to treat it as of no great consequence, is likely to have problems.

A final point here: actually using development as an incentive – 'If you do so and so, I will send you on that course you want to attend' – needs care. On the one hand you might link training activities, making completing some simple form of development, a prerequisite for attending a course. On the other, linking attendance to the achievement of some unrelated target might make it seem that development is not really important. It might seem so if it appears not that the development is something that *should* be done, rather that it is something it might be nice to do. A careful balance is necessary here.

a development culture

At this stage, having said something about why every manager should have a positive attitude towards training, the wider aspects of the view taken within and around an organisation must be considered. It obviously helps if *everyone* in the organisation feels development is necessary and important. As has been said, this feeling will, in all likelihood, exist – people want personal development. It will be more in evidence if people believe that the organisation has a genuine culture of development. The two things reinforce one another.

A positive development culture will help ensure people:

■ take training and development seriously;
■ give the necessary time to it;
■ play a part in identifying what should be done (and how);
■ work at learning from it and use new skills appropriately.

This process must be fostered on a continuing basis. In other words eyes must be kept on the ball of training if it is to be built into ongoing operations in a way that maximises the results it brings. How is this done? In a word: through *communications*.

There are a variety of ways in which the activity of an organisation provides opportunities to build the development culture. Examples include:

■ staff job appraisal procedures;
■ internal communication (from memo to e-mail);
■ noticeboards;
■ training rooms and libraries;
■ newsletters;
■ feedback procedures (eg debriefings and course evaluation forms);

▓ staff and departmental meetings;

▓ annual reports (and other annual reporting procedures).

Together all these and more provide opportunities to engage in a dialogue – a process of communication that continually mentions training. Here the case for training can be made, the results of training reported and new training initiatives planned and flagged. It can be a two-way process, canvassing ideas and suggestions as much as reporting what goes on.

Every manager can usefully play a part in such a process. You need to watch for opportunities; indeed, perhaps you need to actively plan to take an ongoing initiative. These things are helped in a powerful way if there is a commitment from the top of the organisation. If you are lucky, senior managers in your own organisation will champion the development cause. If this does not happen, you may need to direct communication to these levels in order to influence matters.

the range of development methods

If you are reading this book (well, you must be – at least in part!) then you are involved in an element of development activity. Self-development is part of the overall process. Similarly, if you let someone else read it – or, as a manager, recommend or insist on it – you are contributing to the development of others. Actually, hang onto your copy and get them to buy their own, every little royalty helps and... but I digress.

The point is, first, that development encompasses some very simple methodology. None the worse for that – sometimes the simple approach can be highly effective. Second, the escalation from the simplest can take in a whole range of things. Some are still essentially simple. For example, let us go back to reading a book. You can read it, you can pass it on to others, or you can link it to some sort of system (circulating a list of recommended reading). You can continue increasing complexity in this way. Add a target (everyone must read a book each month). Add feedback (what we have learnt from this month's book to be discussed at a staff meeting). Or add a project; for instance, read my book *How to be Better at Writing Reports and Proposals* (also published by Kogan Page) then discuss the next report you write with your manager to see how your style may have adapted and improved. There are a good many options between this sort of thing and something at the other end of the scale: going on a three-month course at an American business school, for instance.

Later, in Chapter 6, a list of various training methodologies is discussed. As well as on-the-job training (see Chapter 4) these include:

- internal (or in-house) courses;
- external courses (public seminars);
- sandwich courses;
- development projects;
- open or distance-learning training;
- computer-presented programmes;
- correspondence courses;
- activity-based training;
- management games and simulations;
- job rotation and shadowing.

To this list can be added some of the techniques of training, such as role-playing or other exercises, which can be used on a course or have a training role in isolation. Thus the range is enormous. At one end we have a group taken out of operational activity for a long period (perhaps many weeks or months) to attend a course; at the other we have the simple reading of an appropriate book.

Always the role of the individual line manager is key.

Progressively we now look at what must be done and how to go about it. The returns can be substantial – a considered approach that does a good job of undertaking the development part of any manager's responsibilities is very worthwhile.

Your attitude and actions with regard to development can literally make the difference between success and failure. You need to see the objective as development designed to achieve excellence in your team. The management fear, mentioned in the introduction, of people being trained who then leave to go elsewhere, needs to be addressed. People will leave; and occasionally it is just inevitable. How much worse, however, to have a group of people so mediocre that none of them is sufficiently competent to *be able* to get another job.

In the next chapter we turn to how to decide just what training and development may be necessary.

assessing competencies

Whatever the job may be, its existence and its working are usually organised and supported by some element of formality. This is necessary if what needs to be done is to be done effectively. The nature of that formality is perhaps best considered if we look at a new situation.

Imagine a growing organisation. In a particular department work volume demands that the number of staff employed be increased. This cannot be done just by pulling in the first person who chances along and saying, 'You fill the gap.' Recruitment and selection processes must be conducted carefully and demand a systematic approach. Many people find the processes involved, including what may sometimes seem like endless interviews, a chore. Worse, they assume they have God-given ability to assess people 'as they walk through the door', as some say. Such a combination of attitudes can be disastrous.

Good recruitment is an essential prerequisite to ensuring that a team functions well. Getting it wrong has dire consequences: certainly the time and cost of getting rid of a candidate who should never have been appointed in the first place, and the dilution of effectiveness (at worst, damage) they may do while in office. It is worth the time and trouble necessary to make the best appointments possible.

Some of the formalities that help are also useful as you move on to consider how to develop an employee who you are happy to retain. These include:

- ▓ *A job definition:* a clear statement of what the job entails, spelling out the objectives, responsibilities and the tasks to be undertaken. Without thinking this through sensible recruitment is impossible.
- ▓ *A candidate profile:* a matching of and clear statement about the kind of person required to do the job (experience, knowledge, qualifications, background, capabilities, etc) complete this picture.

Such may be sufficient to aid the recruitment and selection process, helping to produce any necessary job advertisements (or agency briefings), focus interviews and guide the final selection.

Beyond that, other things may be necessary. For instance, a *job description*, which goes beyond the job definition. It is often more formal and perhaps in many organisations links to Personnel department or Human Resources systems that may demand standard documentation around the organisation. (*Note:* it may also need to be constructed to link appropriately to employment legislation – see page 119 – so that it spells out objectives, standards and such like.

The job description may be regarded as having two distinct roles: a formal one (linked to personnel systems, appraisal, etc) and an informal one, providing a *working* reference, a document that acts, day to day, to help ensure that the correct focus is maintained both in the job and around an organisation or department.

It is good practice to ensure that job descriptions are copied around any group of people whose work overlaps or interrelates in any way. This should include some crossing of levels, so that if you manage other people you should make sure that they see your job description – how else will they fully appreciate the relationship between what each of you does? This may mean preparing a cutdown version of job descriptions, editing them to remove any confidential information (for example about salary or employment grades).

the link with development

Such systems form the foundation of the manager's ability not only to manage but also to develop people. It is essential to have a clear and commonly agreed view of what a particular job entails before you can look at people's ability to carry out their responsibilities, and whether training of some sort is necessary or would help them perform better.

Objectives, for example, must be clear; and it is worth a small digression to spell out just what that means.

job objectives

Objectives should focus attention and effort on the precise nature of the activity required. If objectives are stated too generally they provide inadequate description and, at worst, no direction. Saying that the job of a Customer Relations Executive is to 'liaise with customers' is no more than a glimpse of the obvious; as such it provides little practical help either to the holders of such a job or to their manager.

Objectives must be:

Specific
Measurable
Achievable
Realistic
Timed

Many refer to this as making objectives SMART, the word being taken from the initial letters of the words above. Being *specific* and *measurable* go together, and often mean putting some numbers against the objective; in the case of the job mentioned above maybe 'to handle 100 customer telephone calls a day'. This is a start, though it can be extended, for instance to add more quantitative information such as 'with 70 per cent resulting in an order', or more: specifying the nature and minimum value of the orders.

Achievable means that it can be done – 500 calls in a day might be beyond anyone. The number could be selected to stretch people, but must be possible. *Realistic* means desirable, something from which the organisation will benefit. For example, it would not be realistic to keep customers on the telephone for too long: even if they enjoy a chat it is not productive (so again numbers could be added and made to reflect factors of this sort).

Timing is always important, and it may be necessary to link this to other standards in a variety of ways. Here, for instance, timing could encompass daily activity through to annual achievement and also to output: 'resolving all complaints within 24 hours' perhaps.

creating a development plan

A development plan may be necessary for the whole organisation. Drawn up by the HR department, or by consultants, it should reflect the requirements of individual parts of the organisation (managers must be consulted). It can then help plan and chart progress across the whole organisation. This does not in any way absolve the individual manager from the responsibility of having an agreed plan for each and every individual who reports to him or her. This plan need not be complex.

But why is it necessary? First, because even with a modest number of people reporting to you it is not possible to commit everything to memory (you surely have enough day-to-day operational matters to concern yourself with). Second, it bestows importance on the whole area of development and on the plan for each person. Seeing that their training plan is the subject of some concern to you will be regarded as motivational.

More of individual development plans anon. First, because development plans are, most often, an extension of the job appraisal process, a word about that is appropriate here, too.

job appraisal

Like recruitment, this is an area some (many?) managers find awkward or distasteful. It is only so if the system being used is inappropriate, or perhaps if the reasons for it, or the way to undertake it, are not fully explained or appreciated.

In fact, appraisal is a real opportunity, for manager and staff alike. And sound training and development plans are inextricably linked with it. It is difficult to imagine development running very well alongside an inadequate appraisal process. If your staff do not see appraisal in the right light, it is no good blaming central departments or processes – the responsibility is yours (though perhaps you should be assisted by others in the organisation in the task of explaining). Consider for a moment: what exactly are job appraisals for?

Put simply, past performance is reviewed through appraisal in order to help make future performance better. It is an ongoing process, of course, and the (often annual) appraisal is only the most formal manifestation of it. As a manager, your performance (and perhaps the tenure of your own job too!) is dependent upon your team performing well. Appraisal is a prime opportunity to help secure that future performance.

Specifically the purpose of appraisal meetings is to:

▨ review individuals' past performance;
▨ plan their future work and role;
▨ set specific individual goals for the future;
▨ agree and create individual ownership of such goals;
▨ identify development needs and set up development activity;
▨ carry out on-the-spot coaching;
▨ obtain feedback;
▨ reinforce or extend reporting relationships;
▨ act as a catalyst to delegation;
▨ focus on long-term career progression;
▨ motivate.

The above, to which you could maybe add, are not mutually exclusive. Appraisals are usually trying to address a number of different things, but development should always rank high among them.

This is not the place to review the whole process of appraisal, but with an eye on development you should certainly take on board certain key approaches. You need to:

▨ Ensure your people understand what appraisal is for, not least how it can help them.
▨ Encourage (insist?) that they prepare for appraisal and aim to get the most out of it (this means not just having a think before the meeting, but running an 'appraisals file', collecting information and documents through the year – a year is, after all, a long period to recall – and considering progressively what the events of the year mean for appraisal).
▨ Set, and issue ahead of the meeting, a clear agenda (maybe in consultation with the appraisee) and make clear the importance of developmental issues.
▨ Encourage the appraisee to talk (after all, you are trying to find out about them – they should hold the floor as it were for more than 50 per cent of the time, during which your job is to listen).

■ Focus on the future. A constructive appraisal is not an opportunity to lay blame (well, this may be appropriate sometimes) but to plan for the future, picking up both positive and negative events and linking them to the future. Again, more than 50 per cent of the discussion should look ahead – maybe much more.

In this way you can ensure that the meeting will be useful and it will be seen as useful, before, during and after it is held. Always bear in mind that people are not only concerned about their progress; they will increasingly want to get the best from appraisals. There is plenty of guidance for them (for example my own book, *30 Minutes Before Your Job Appraisal*, published by Kogan Page), and you should not underestimate their knowledge or expectations.

the development dimension

Discussion of development should be a key part of the appraisal meeting. Several factors need addressing:

■ *Identifying development needs:* this is clearly the first stage. It stems both from the activity of the year immediately past and from further back. A project that the appraisee executed during the year may have highlighted something that needs attention: a skills deficiency of some sort perhaps.

■ *Agreeing development needs:* it is not enough for a manager simply to say, 'You need training'. The individual must recognise both the weakness (or gap; it may be something in which they never needed to have competence in the past), and agree the need to correct it.

■ *Discussing suitable action to correct the situation:* this might be linked to an agreed decision – 'So, you attend the next course on that' – or to future action (beyond the appraisal meeting) – 'Let's find out what sort of course would suit and talk about it again in a month or so'. Action must be specific here, making clear who will do what and setting deadlines (and sometimes budgets).

▓ *Taking action now:* time will preclude all but the most straightforward things being addressed within the appraisal meeting itself, but sometimes a brief word is all that is necessary.

▓ *Recording conclusions and linking to an action plan:* development action must not be forgotten (even in the heat of operational pressures), so clear notes need to be made. Matters may have to be summarised in the overall report that often follows appraisal meetings. An *action* note is important too, however. A memo, or e-mail, to the appraisee can confirm matters. Moreover, the manager needs a personal note to act as a reminder. This can take many forms, such as a diary note (electronic or otherwise). The importance of development prompts many managers to keep a current record sheet (this could be a page for each person they manage in a system such as Filofax, or a format on screen in a computer system or electronic personal organiser).

The record – which effectively forms the individual development plan referred to earlier – will have three dimensions of development to note. First, it should list the needs identified (for example: *skills of formal presentation* must be strengthened). Then it should list the action agreed (*attending a course*: though this could well be preceded or followed by other action). And third it should note – and link to the diary – any ongoing review, consultation or coaching sessions that are necessary between manager and subordinate (or indeed that will involve anyone else).

This kind of record can show the state of play at any

particular moment. It can be updated, amended or extended as required (or as agreed by both parties) and act as a catalyst, ensuring that action follows the formal appraisal meeting and that what needs to be done – both immediately afterwards and in the longer term – does actually occur.

Thus the record and the appraisal, and the other communications they prompt, combine to produce a rolling plan that creates the continuous focus on the development that is needed. Working in this kind of way also guarantees that things will not be forgotten and demonstrates an interest in, or commitment to, the member of staff concerned. Without this, what may well start as enthusiasm can quickly deteriorate into disappointment and disillusionment, which reduces motivation and dilutes performance.

a cycle of improvement

Thus managers have a responsibility to address the question of performance in the job of everyone reporting to them, and to continue doing so over time. In the first place it is important to define the job and recruit and select someone truly suitable to fill it. Then the performance has to be regularly reviewed, and the job appraisal process puts a formality on this. Implementing the plan that stems from this activity is an ongoing process. It needs to be set up in a way that focuses attention on it, and linked to systems that make it happen.

Levels of competence are not something to be addressed once in a while in an ad hoc way. Creating and maintaining competence is at the heart of any manager's job.

the development task

It has been said already that training and development should be a continuous process. The last chapter looked at recruitment as a starting point to this process, at the way in which formalities such as job descriptions help, and at the overall role of job appraisal. Here we look more at the day-to-day job of development and the ways of accurately identifying where exactly development must be directed.

The manager's job is to ensure the right performance from others, those reporting to him or her, and to make sure this is maintained. Realistically, both what people do and how they do it varies over time. Sometimes this has nothing to do with their level of skills and overall competence: people do more or less because of a variety of factors, and other influences from organisation to motivation are instrumental in controlling this. People's actual ability to do their job is key, however, and this needs constant monitoring.

the development gap

Like apple pie any development may be regarded as a 'good

thing'. Indeed that may be; it should after all do good. In addition, as we will see, some training and development may be unspecific and have general, long-term aims and be none the less appropriate for that. But there is a need in most organisations to look at the current situation and the short term, and to use development to help achieve aims that stem from business plans describing the next period (whatever that may be defined as being in an organisation). The process of looking at this and deciding what needs to be done can be tackled systematically, as follows:

▨ *Examine job descriptions:* this allows you to review the levels of knowledge and skills that a particular *job* demand, and the attitudes required of the person who does it. This states the ideal and the current position and is not, at this stage, linked to the individual currently doing the job.

▨ *Examine the person:* this enables you to look, alongside the ideal, at what the situation actually is currently. How do the knowledge, skills and attitudes of the individual stack up alongside what the job demands? This information comes from observation of the person, his or her performance, and results. Formal appraisal is a key part of this, as is – as we will see – other, less formal, evaluation.

▨ *Look to the future:* before reaching any conclusions from the process described so far, you need also to think ahead, again focusing on the job. What will the job demand in future that will be different from the current situation? What developments (in the organisation, in technology, in the market and expectation of customers – and more) are coming? Specifically, what new skills, knowledge or attitudes will be necessary, and how will existing ones need to change?

▨ *Defining the gap:* together two factors coming from the above may define a gap: the combination of any shortfall in current levels of competence plus the need to add to this in future. This is the so-called *training (or development) gap* and gives you the area towards which development must be directed with any individual.

Of course, the picture produced may be fine; no immediate action may be necessary. The reality is most likely that some action – major or minor – is required. If so you need a plan of action to deal with implementation. Again viewing this systematically provides a simple checklist approach as to what to do:

▓ *List what needs to be addressed:* include whatever is identified, from minor matters that need only a small input to new skills that must be approached from square one.

▓ *Rate the list in terms of priorities:* in most organisations resources (time, money and training facilities) are finite. It is unlikely to be possible to do everything that might be desirable instantly, and impossible to select what comes first or should be postponed, without some clear thinking-through of priorities.

▓ *Put some timing to it:* having established priorities you need to consider when things are to be done. What is urgent? What can be postponed without causing problems and what might be addressed in parts? (Perhaps something can be done early on, but action also planned to follow up and complete the training task later.)

▓ *Consider the method most suitable:* this needs to relate quite closely to timing. With a list of desirable training and priorities set, you need to consider exactly how something will be approached (a course, a project, whatever).

▓ *Calculate costs:* this is always an important issue, and realistically may involve some compromise and the balancing of different approaches (more people given at least some training versus fewer people given thorough training, for example).

■ *Link to an action plan:* the net result of these deliberations needs to be documented, and turned into a rolling plan that sets out what will be done, in what way, when and involving whom. This may be recorded in part on a per person basis as suggested in the previous chapter.

In this kind of way training and development activities can be considered, worked out and scheduled on a basis that makes sense. Such consideration must:

■ relate closely to operational matters;
■ link and liaise as necessary with any appropriate central department or manager (eg a training manager) – not least to draw on their experience and expertise;
■ reflect suitable consultation with the staff involved, a process that stems originally from job appraisal discussions.

To make such a process possible presupposes being well informed about the people concerned and their performance; this, in turn, presupposes some evaluation through the year.

evaluating throughout the year

Appraisal is a formal process. It was mentioned earlier and is likely to happen, on at least an annual basis, in any organisation of any size (employment legislation alone in the UK has exerted considerable pressure for this to be so). However, most managers would concede that they would know precious little about their staff if that was the only occasion during the year on which their performance was discussed.

Other occasions for evaluation need to be found, and a basis for using them effectively worked out. Some of these will be very informal and need no documenting here. Others will be incorporated into occasions that exist primarily for other purposes, such as departmental or project meetings.

Some should be specifically for the purpose of evaluation. To be able to do this you need to be sure that:

- there is a common understanding of the job in question (this is one of the rationales for the formality of job descriptions and for their being regarded as *working* documents) so that the detail can be discussed;
- there is similar understanding of any targets involved;
- such understanding is reflected in an agreed system for evaluation.

If this is the case then discussion about the job can flow easily. Such discussion is often best preceded by observation; you need to look not only at *what* is being achieved, but also *how* it is being done. The latter is the only way of linking to skills and techniques and seeing how they are being deployed. Remember that simply looking at results, for example the number of things done or something that is recorded, does not tell you *how* things were done or, of itself, show a possibility of change and improvement.

Practice varies in exactly how such evaluation sessions are conducted. Some managers favour a very informal approach, others something more formal and properly documented. What is important is that there is a continuum of activity. Some action may consist of no more than a few words in passing, while some will be short sessions maybe linking an element of evaluation to projects or other discussions. On other occasions a dedicated session will focus exclusively on evaluation.

Even if you opt for the informal, the way the session might be documented makes its precise nature clear. There are two elements to have in mind during evaluation.

First, *the activities that the job entails:* here you need to tease things out so that *all* the constituent elements of a job are 'on the table' as it were. Consider staff dealing with customers on the telephone: if they are handling a complaint, say, they need a good telephone manner. This in turn necessitates a whole list of things being done right: they have to be polite, get the burden of the complaint clear, appear sympathetic to give confidence, calm down people who are angry and more – much more. Their effectiveness is dependent on the totality of this. Individual elements are important, and weakness in one may well dilute the effectiveness of the whole.

Evaluation needs to look at *how* these things are being done. It is insufficient just to say that on the whole customers are happy with how things are done; to deal with any weakness you have to be clear *why* it is occurring, perhaps in this case because of poor listening skills. Similarly, and just as important, if you are to build on strengths you need to evaluate. Let me emphasise this last point. Evaluating should be as much about building on strengths as identifying and correcting weaknesses. This is a factor that helps make the whole process acceptable.

The relationship with job descriptions is clear and may form the starting point for such a list, though for evaluation purposes more detail may be necessary. The point is that both manager and staff need to be clear precisely what it is that is being evaluated.

Second, *the level of performance:* here you need some sort of scale on which to mark people. This kind of thing often exists in formal appraisal documentation, indeed that may help produce what you need here. Simplicity is the key. You need a rating scale. An even number of ratings is best (avoiding the temptation to mark down the middle too much), perhaps four or six levels. This might be stated as *Satisfactory, Above average, Below average,* and *Unsatisfactory.* The words are largely unimportant. You might equally use a scale of: 1, 2, 3 and 4 (as long as everyone is clear which end is which!) On the other hand, sometimes you may want to put a description to the ratings: for instance that someone always does something, nearly always does it and so on.

The marking here is not something that needs to be completed comprehensively every time. With a long list of factors this might not even be practical. So different things may need addressing on different occasions. Nor is it a system the results of which need to sit forever on the record. It is simply a spur to action.

Imagine four rating scales: there is effectively a line down the middle. Marking on the top two might be taken to mean 'no action', though there might be something to say about either. Marking on the lower two means performance is such that remedial action is necessary, especially on the lowest. And this prompting of action is what you are after. Evaluation prompts a constructive dialogue about performance, and the rating element of it prompts action if and where necessary.

Many managers implement this sort of activity with no actual completion of a form (though a checklist might help). Certainly many would say that, beyond a reminder of action to follow, any documentation that is used should not be kept on the record (though some factors may need noting separately on an individual's file).

Overall, the intention is to prompt and channel constructive dialogue aimed at fine-tuning performance, and to do so in a way that is acceptable and effective. It is an opportunity to motivate when things go well, or are made to do so following action. It links to straightforward counselling and on-the-job training (more of which later). And it can link to formal development activity too.

Regular inputs of this sort need not be disproportionately time-consuming and, effectively done, can pay dividends in terms of improved performance.

the effect on the individual

The key to making evaluation work is that it is a practical process. First, people must understand the job they are employed to undertake and understand, in detail, what needs to be done to enable them to make that job effective.

Second, they must see the need for good performance and thus the need to ensure it happens. Then they must find the process of evaluation and its link with developmental activity (whether simple or more elaborate) to be useful. If the discussions it prompts are fair, constructive and, above all, *if people find it helps them* (maybe making the job easier or more satisfying), then the process will be accepted. More than that, the existence of such activity will be found motivational.

Managers must set it up, explain it and undertake it in the right way. If it is made effective then it can become a regular, inherent element of the management process – one that builds on strengths, nips weaknesses in the bud and fine-tunes performance on a continuing basis.

There is one more advantage to all this which, at the end of the day, is perhaps more important than anything else.

creating the right habit

How is it some people excel at what they do? There are probably many reasons (including their willingness to take advantage of help given, as we have been discussing). One reason in particular is paramount. It is the ability to undertake self-analysis linked to fine-tuning. People who understand what they have to do and what makes it work well, and who *consider what they do and how they can improve it still more*, will always have a head start on those who just go through the motions.

Some people have this habit of thinking about what they do.

They handle a complaint, or whatever, and say to themselves afterwards: 'How did that go? What might I have done differently? What must I keep in mind for next time?' and so on. It makes a difference – they resolve to act differently in future, and do so. This sort of conscious self-analysis is invaluable. Done on a regular basis – and we may only be talking about a few seconds' thought sometimes – it can lead to resolve and action, which progressively build performance, and do so regularly and *on a self-contained basis*, without a prompt from a manager.

A manager's work with people can certainly act to improve performance, and will do so if it is well executed. But you are not at people's elbow every moment of the day. The result that will influence performance most, therefore, is the way in which such activity can act to develop such a habit in people; a practice that allows them to evaluate and improve their own performance in the manager's absence. And what you do with people in evaluation, and the action that follows it, can be used to instil such a habit – and that is perhaps its most valuable result.

Some of the thoughts expressed here are picked up later, especially in Chapter 5 where the topic of on-the-job training relates directly to the processes described here. At this point let us be clear: development is dependent on a clear understanding of what must be done – no one can improve performance if they are uncertain of what it is or of precisely how it is produced. With a firm factual basis for enhancing performance, refreshed by regular evaluation, and ultimately by self-evaluation, and with an acceptance that development should take place – it can be made to happen.

Much of what then needs to be done fits closely with operational activity for both manager and staff; certainly that is true of the topic for Chapter 4.

4

delegation as an aid to development

At first thought delegation does not seem to be automatically linked to development. But it depends how you look at it. Certainly staff must actually be able to do something that is delegated to them; indeed their not being able to do something is often the reason why delegation does *not* take place. Conversely, if you want to develop someone, what better way than planning to delegate something and then making sure that they are suitably equipped to do it and do it right? The reason for focusing on delegation in this chapter is to look at it as a regular mechanism to ensure development; to view it, in fact, as an option in actively prompting learning. There are other advantages too, but we are getting ahead of ourselves. Let us define terms.

Delegation is more than simply the allocation of work. All managers delegate; there may be a daily need to decide who does what. But delegation is, to risk being pedantic, 'the art and act of giving a subordinate the necessary authority to make decisions and carry out action in a specified area of *our* work'. It implies the handover of tasks and responsibilities by the manager, so that they are left – permanently for the future – to someone else to do. Well, nothing is *forever*, of course, but the point is that a task is repositioned on an ongoing basis, not simply changed momentarily, say to cover a holiday absence.

the benefits of delegation

Given the definition above, what can delegation achieve overall? There are several potential results, including, first, and especially relevant here, that it creates, for those to whom matters are delegated, an opportunity for development and accelerated experience. In addition:

- It builds morale (precisely because it opens the door to development, and because it can provide immediate variety and long-term opportunity) and gives job satis-faction and – all being well – a sense of achievement that is motivational.
- It builds team well-being (again a reflection of the motivational effect above).
- It allows those delegating to concentrate time and effort on those aspects of their job that are key to the achievement of objectives (reflecting the 80/20 rule that a few things give rise to most of the desired results).
- It can bring a more considered or creative approach to bear, prompting a view that may avoid other distrac-tions and allow a broad brush or longer-term perspec-tive on key issues.

As well as making clear how development is assisted, it is worth noting that one of the other significant results directly affects the person doing the delegating. It offers a way to improve *your* performance.

So, if delegation brings advantage to one and all, why do so many people moan that 'My manager won't delegate anything?'

the reasons why delegation may be avoided

No one wants a boss who hangs onto everything, involves no one in anything (especially anything interesting) and who, as a result, is seen as generally secretive and not the ideal manager for whom to work. So why does delegation so often seem to present difficulties? It can be curiously difficult even for effective managers to delegate as readily and often as they know they should.

There are several reasons, for instance:

■ something may go wrong;
■ time may then be wasted sorting it out;
■ mistakes may be blamed, not on whoever takes the action, but on the manager instigating it.

There is another, different, reason worth separate comment: the manager fears, not that the other person will not cope, but that they will cope *too well*, that they may *improve* the method, that they will do something more quickly, more thoroughly and better in some way than he or she did.

The more honest among us may privately admit the truth of this; certainly it seems as common as the fear that people will not cope, even if that is sometimes volunteered first.

Nevertheless, even if this is, in a sense, an instinctive reaction, it should not put you off delegating – the rewards are just too great to miss. Even if this 'fear' proves correct and something is improved, so much to the good. The amount you can do if you delegate successfully is way beyond the improvement in productivity that you can hope to achieve in almost any other way.

This is actually one of the key ways in which progress is made in an organisation as new people, new ways and new thinking are brought to bear on tasks. Without this process, organisations would be stultified and largely unable to cope with change. In any case, in the event of change coming from those to whom you delegate, there is no reason to feel bad. It is your selection, development, counselling and management that create and maintain a strong effective team; and this is something for which you *can* rightly take the credit.

Still, delegation does bring inherent risks that must be countered and we will look at how this can be done before returning specifically to development.

minimising the risk

There is always the possibility that delegation will not work. After all, it passes on the 'right to be wrong' as it were, by putting someone else in the driving seat. So misjudgements must be avoided particularly with regard to the choice of:

- ■ what is delegated;
- ■ to whom matters are delegated;
- ■ how the process is carried out.

Without this, the result may be that mistakes are made (with whatever consequences they may have) and time must be spent – wasted – putting things right. In these circumstances, not least given the objectives, the person to whom something has been delegated may feel let down and demotivated and certainly the chances of him or her learning very much (except perhaps to be wary in future) are slight.

So, the net intention must be to find a way forward that minimises the inherent risk by:

1. *Selecting tasks that are suitable for delegation:* for most managers, in most jobs, there will be certain things that should sensibly *not* be top of the list to be delegated, but where responsibility should stay

with the manager. Such could routinely include matters:
- that are key to overall results generation or control;
- of staff discipline;
- that are contentious in some way (eg staff grievances);
- confidential at the level delegation takes place (though, incidentally, it is a good rule to minimise the amount that must be kept confidential).

However, doubtless such a list will leave plenty of other tasks from which to choose.

2. *Picking suitable people to whom to delegate:* this means asking questions such as:
- Have they undertaken similar tasks in the past?
- Do they have the necessary knowledge, experience and capability?
- How much can they cope with at once?
- Is some prior training (of whatever sort) necessary first?
- Do they want to embrace the change?
- Will they be acceptable to others with whom they will cross paths in undertaking the task?
- Will it be perceived as fair by their peers that they get the chance (or can it be explained as such)?
- Does their selection make possible any particular positive changes that are desired?

Thereafter the greatest guarantee of success is clear communication. This must be carried out as widely as necessary. Others may need to know what is going on, who is now doing what and why; they may subsequently have to put their trust in the person concerned. Such communication must spell out details regarding authority and responsibility and, above all, must make clear to the individual why the task is necessary and why he or she is doing it. He or she needs, after all, to be confident, after any briefing, about making a good job of it.

Remember, too, that ultimately (perhaps after a successful test) permanent amendment may need to be made to systems, procedures and such documents as job descriptions.

3. *Development to make effective delegation possible:* here lies the heart of why delegation is so important to development. From an assessment of the tasks and the individual you need to identify any necessary preliminary development and consider how to action it.

Consider an example. Say you wish to delegate some project – undertaking an analysis of productivity in a certain operation for instance (the details are not important). Let us say also that the person selected to carry out the work is well able to do what is necessary; all that is needed is a small briefing. On the other hand, the project must conclude (as must other similar projects that could in turn form a regular part of their future work) with a formal presentation. This is not something the person has done, or indeed in which he or she believes they have an inherent ability. Some sort of training is necessary.

This might take many forms: attending a course, coupled with planning and rehearsing the first one with the manager – whatever. Methods are covered elsewhere; here all that matters is to see that appropriate development action needs to be decided on as an inherent part of the delegation process. It is also important that it is carried out as, but ahead of, action being taken.

monitoring progress

There is another stage, also with development possibilities, that must be considered. Once something has been passed over to another, keeping in touch can easily be forgotten. Equally, actually keeping in touch can present problems. It must be done, in a word, *carefully*. If it is not then it will smack of interference and the whole process may be doomed. The simplest way to monitor in an acceptable way is to build in any necessary checks at the time of the original briefing and handover. From the beginning, ask for interim reports at logical points (maybe these can be described as an opportunity for the other person to check progress rather than vice versa).

Do not simply arrive unannounced alongside someone's desk and ask to see how things stand (they may be at an awkward stage). Let them bring things to you, and do so at a pre-agreed time. If they have been well briefed, know what is expected and what standards apply, then they can deliver in a way that either duplicates past practice or which brings something new to the activity. Either may be appropriate in the short term, though, as nothing is the right way forever, new thinking is usually to be encouraged once the person has a real handle on the basics.

Two specific points are relevant here. First, *development* may be inherent to the process. A project involving a presentation, for example, might be set up so that the necessary development, or some of it, is enmeshed within the project with time being taken for a counselling session as the presentation is prepared or rehearsed. Second, *letting go*. It may be necessary (not least to learning) to let things proceed, to bite your tongue and resist taking the whole matter back or interfering in some way to 'get it right'. It is especially tempting to pitch in if you see things being done differently; remember that – despite this – the outcome may be perfectly satisfactory.

Delegation is no simple matter. There is a systematic way of going about it, but the ultimate results make all the effort worthwhile, and not just in time terms but in terms of growth and development within the workplace.

evaluating the process

There is still a final stage to consider. You need to know how things have gone (give it a little while for everything to have fallen into place), and thus a number of questions need to be asked. These can usefully include:

- Has the task been completed satisfactorily?
- Did it take an acceptable amount of time?
- Does it indicate the person could take on more?
- What else might be similarly delegated?
- What effect did the process have on others, eg seeing this, do others want more delegated to them?
- Are any changes necessary to procedures or systems now a new person is charged with the task on an ongoing basis?
- Has any new, revised or adapted methodology been created and, if so, with what implications?

In addition, do not forget to ask yourself:

- How has this affected *you*? (What have you done with the time saved, for instance?) There is little merit in delegating if you end up submerged in detail and the change makes no real difference to the key tasks for which you still have responsibility.
- What have you achieved from a *development* point of view? For instance, to continue our example, if presentation skills have been (or are beginning to be) developed, what does that mean in terms of the future of the person concerned?

If the exercise was successful, then there may be directions indicated for the future; the advantages may be more than one-off. Similarly, should the process not be a success, questions should be asked about what went wrong and they need to address both sides, asking not just what someone did wrong, or perhaps misunderstood, but also raising such questions as how thoroughly you, in fact, briefed that person. Many constructive lessons may come from the process. Indeed it is important for all concerned to learn from the experience; testing what you delegate, to whom, and seeking the best way of handling the process is very worthwhile. If you develop good habits in this way it can pay dividends over time.

People tend to carry out with greatest enthusiasm and care about those things for which they have responsibility. In delegating you pass on the opportunity for additional responsibility (though strictly speaking responsibility can only be taken, you cannot force it on people) and you must also pass on the authority to act. Delegation produces challenges, and of course there are risks. Normally, however, people will strive hard to make it work and the failure rate, at least of well-considered delegation, will be low. It is not just a way of shedding chores (indeed high on the list of things to delegate may be things among those that you enjoy doing most), it is a process with potential rewards that can hardly be overrated.

As Theodore Roosevelt once said: 'The best executive is the one who has sense enough to pick good men to do what he wants done, and the self-restraint to keep from meddling with them while they do it'. Sound advice, even today (when, in a politically correct world, we should perhaps substitute the word 'people').

As has been said, the development dimension to delegation is one of considerable importance in its own right. To summarise, it:

- provides regular development opportunities;
- positions development as an integral part of the operational task of 'getting things done' and thus makes it relevant;
- makes learning, and a commitment to learn, more

likely (as the person wants to succeed and perform satisfactorily);

▓ can be linked into ongoing training, certainly into existing training plans, not least in a way that demonstrates management's commitment to the other person;

▓ promotes the development culture around the team (or organisation) and adds to positive motivational influences.

The interface between the tasks to be carried out, delegation and development is one that can have considerable effect operationally, not least in terms of productivity (delegation saves time), but also on what is done and, longer term, how it is done. As people's skills evolve and extend it is often here that they get their first test.

on-the-job training

Here we review a major method influencing development, and one that can be used regularly. The phrase 'on-the-job training' implies a range of activity, ways of working with a member of your staff that can be integrated into the day-to-day activity of you both. It is at once largely low key and highly effective. Like so much else in management, however, its effectiveness can easily be diluted by an ad hoc approach, and in part this chapter is designed to set out something of the systematic approach that can make it work best.

This aspect of development is something that is personally applied. You have control, and the effect is immediate. It is thus something that is an inherent part of the manager–subordinate relationship. It should strengthen this, have a positive motivational effect and – of course above all – act to improve performance.

the target of on-the-job training

It is worth considering in turn two different categories of people: new and existing – more experienced – staff.

new staff

Here on-the-job training is part of the induction process. Clearly it is important when people are first appointed that they understand the job and are able to undertake all the various activities that make it up. With internal appointments less briefing may be necessary, though you should not automatically assume that the knowledge and skill someone gleaned in another department are exactly what they will need while working for you.

More so with external appointments: people may have a skill but be used to applying it in a rather different way from what is now necessary. For example, someone dealing with people on the telephone may have good telephone skills but be used only to dispensing information. If a new job demands, say, offering advice then skills may need some adaptation. Such transitions may not be complicated, but they need to be dealt with and dealt with promptly and certainly.

At an early stage in someone's work with you there are a number of ways in which your input to their development can be beneficial. These include helping in:

- establishing skills on the right basis as a foundation of the way someone will work during their tenure in a particular job;
- developing good working habits, which in turn act to produce consistency of performance;
- producing attitudes to, and understanding of, what needs to be done so that a person is inherently likely to be more self-sufficient in what he or she does;
- establishing an attention to detail, for example in following prescribed systems, that make for precision of work in whatever way is required;
- building confidence quickly in what they do and in a way that affects their ability to work effectively.

All such intentions can be important, and if a new employee is set up right, so to speak, he or she will be better able to operate as required thereafter. Attitude and activity go together. For instance, if you want someone to adopt a creative approach, to think about what goes on and how it might be improved, rather than simply follow a slavish pattern, then this is best established early on.

experienced staff

Here the requirement is rather different. Even when performance is good, there is a need to fine-tune skills and to add them. There is also a need for briefing to continue, as policy and practice change over time. This – coupled with the sensible attitude that even the best performance can be improved – means that development, certainly in many things, never stops. Yet experienced people can easily resent training, seeing some of it at least as a negative reflection on their current skills. Good on-the-job training, and indeed the routine of its use, can make ongoing development acceptable and thus, in turn, allow it to have a more certain effect.

Where training and development in specific skills are involved there is a need to consider carefully exactly what is needed.

defining the development task

Whatever is being contemplated, your view of it must be clear. Specifically this means defining:

▓ *What* the individual must be able to do, or – let us be necessarily pedantic – *exactly* what they have to do and how they should go about it. Sometimes this means learning to follow an exact procedure;

alternatively it might mean adopting a less rigid, but specific approach. And it could mean both. Someone who must handle complaints, for instance, must deal with them systematically (if certain things are not done in a certain order it may well make what can be a difficult situation worse). But they must also deal with them in a way that is tailored to the individual complainant; indeed anything less can make it seem that no individual concern is being expressed, and it seems as if, 'This is how they deal with it to fob us off.'

▓ *The conditions under which performance must be achieved.* On-the-job training must reflect the real world. It is no good someone being able to do something right only in highly artificial conditions; they must be able to do it as it needs to be done. Consider a specific example. I am involved in a good deal of sales training. Sales people need to be able to communicate persuasively (and more besides, but let's keep it simple). They not only need to be able to communicate in this way, but to do so in a meeting or contact of appropriate duration. Sometimes this time can be very short. In the world of pharmaceuticals, sales people calling on doctors must often do so between their appointments with patients. In a meeting designed to inform and update a doctor about their drugs (what in the industry is referred to as *detailing*) they have, in the UK at least, an average of around four minutes to do so. Someone who is wonderfully persuasive – eventually – simply cannot do the job. The short duration is a 'given'. Operating that way goes with the territory as they say, and subsequently any training directed at this area must reflect that reality. Any job doubtless has such factors associated with it.

▓ *The link with standards.* The duration of sales visit referred to above may always be short, but it is not an exact duration. Sometimes there is a precision that must be reflected in work and training alike and this links to targets or standards that form part of the job description. So, for example, standards specifying the number of customer calls to be handled, on average, in the call centres so beloved of our financial institutions these days, have a mandatory impact on the job – and on development undertaken to equip people to do it.

Thus, development can best proceed with clear thinking in these sorts of ways and with clear objectives resulting from them (for exactly what is implied by 'clear objectives', see page 14). Given a discrete on-the-job development objective, what is then necessary is a systematic way of approaching it.

a systematic approach

To be effective, and to get things done productively because time is always of the essence, it is best to approach things systematically. Taking things from scratch, for most tasks the following makes good sense:

- First, *describe the task*. Tell people what needs to be done. Normally this means what is says: telling them verbally, though description could be enhanced in other ways (ranging from a checklist in a manual to a tutorial on a computer screen).
- Second, *demonstrate what must be done*. This is designed to reinforce description and help ensure that the person is entirely clear what he or she is expected to do. With many things the manager will be able to do this personally, though it is possible with some technical tasks that certain demonstrations might be better done by someone else. Do beware here, however, of assuming that someone who can do something, even who can do it with a degree of excel-

lence, is automatically able to describe to others *how* they do it. Thinking this is most often a fallacy, and the technique of sitting down one person with another, more expert, and simply saying, 'Watch', is suspect. Certainly care is needed with what is still sometimes referred to as the 'sitting by Nellie' way of training; it can sometimes simply be a way of managers avoiding their responsibilities.

A process of prompting questions should accompany the two stages above to be sure that the person is now clear what is required. Such questions must not be censorious. If you say something like, 'Right, I'm sure that's clear, any questions?' there is a danger that people will be put off asking anything for fear that you will think less well of them if they do. As any confusion can lengthen the whole process unnecessarily care is needed here.

▨ *Allow practice.* At this stage the person must be allowed to have a go, with you, the manager, watching. All may be well and no further action may be necessary (maybe a written note of some sort by way of reminder?). But the role of the manager is to watch and to assess how things are done, and sometimes a further stage is called for.

▨ *Provide assistance to get it right.* Here, if necessary, you may need to provide further assistance. Again, care is necessary. An immediate negative response may upset someone and put off the moment when they get the hang of something. It is often best to encourage the other person to analyse what they have done, to prompt them to talk it through. Asking questions such as, 'How did that go?', 'Did you get everything right?', 'How might you have done it differently?', can act to bring out shortfalls. Then a second layer of questions may be necessary: 'Why did that happen?', 'How can you make sure it doesn't happen next time?', and so on. It may seem quicker just to say: 'No, do it this way.' But it is less effective in prompting learning than is counselling a person to tease out the solution themselves; one that will then be remembered and used next time.

■ *Practice again (and again)*. Sometimes further practice is necessary. This might mean doing it once more with your supervision, or it might be better to disappear and leave them to practise further quietly on their own. You might set a time on this: 'I'll pop back in an hour and see how you're doing.' Or you might leave it with them: 'Let me know if you have any more problems'; whatever seems appropriate.

■ *Encourage throughout the process*. This is important, and may sometimes mean *finding* an opportunity to praise (and perhaps to continue to explain if the task is something no one gets right instantly). A feeling of making progress can shorten the learning process and thus the time all this takes.

Note: in approaching the task reviewed above, remember to keep the perspective of the trainees firmly in mind. What is obvious to you may not be obvious to them. You have to remember their frame of reference. Ask yourself: what experience do they have of this? If none, can it be equated to something else, which they do have experience of and which exhibits similar characteristics? Such questions and their answers can help you position things in an appropriate way. Remember, too, that if you have to go back to basics this may be only because they lack certain experience, so do not make someone feel bad about it.

Similarly you need to bear in mind the habits of the past. Sometimes these can be very strong and difficult to break, even when it is well accepted that they should change. One area where I notice this regularly is in dealing with training in business writing skills. People may want to change, but habits of writing are deeply ingrained and this fact needs to be accommodated when new approaches are mooted.

Here is an example relating to a simple, specific development task, showing how it can be tackled.

on-the-job training in action: example

Here we review the principles against a particular task, the interactive communication involved in *handling complaints* as might have to be undertaken by various categories of support staff.

1. *Select an example:* this might specify the nature of the complaint and the characteristics of the person making it, say on the telephone.
2. *Review background facts:* this might involve looking at policy (money back, no questions asked, or whatever) and the information that would need to be to hand in order to deal effectively with such a complaint (product information, customer order record, etc).
3. *Plan the action necessary:* given the example, planning for contacts which, almost by definition, are unique (and certainly seen as wholly individual by complainants) can be in outline only – but a general view of how such things are handled is nevertheless useful.
4. *Agree the details with the trainee:* if analysis afterwards is going to be useful this is important. Your comments will need to be about what *they* decided and agreed to do, and you do not want them saying something like, 'I never felt it was a good way forward anyway.'
5. *Agree what your role will be:* if training is going to involve observing a real call then whether or not you are available to take over and rescue the situation if

necessary needs to be clear. Remember that unplanned intervention will always upset staff, who will doubtless feel that, whatever the difficulty, they were – *just about to get it right.*

6. *Observe:* watch and listen to how something goes. In the example it might be a real call (you might have to ask to be summoned quickly when the right kind of call comes in); or an expected call to allow it all to be observed (eg making a call to someone who has been promised a call back).

   Here observation needs to address the technical nature of the task to ensure that it is being completed appropriately. In this case it means noting things such as:

   – Did they really listen carefully to what was said?
   – Did they make it clear they were listening?
   – Did they note, accurately, the details referred to during the conversation?
   – Were they suitably sympathetic (while not perhaps accepting blame at this stage)?
   – Did the complaint need clarifying and was that done effectively? (An angry outburst can be difficult to follow, for instance.)
   – Was the complaint summarised to double check that both parties were talking about exactly the same thing?
   – What checks were made on the facts (in files or on screen or whatever)?
   – Was any necessary wait while this was done made acceptable or was there an offer to phone back?
   – What action was suggested or answer given to resolve the problem?
   – Was the way of handling the complaint appropriate (to the customer and the organisation)?
   – Was any necessary apology sincere and appropriate? (And personally put – 'I am sorry' – without the blame being avoided; an apologetic tone may be needed throughout.)

- Was any follow-up action appropriate, made clear and agreed with the customer and noted for future action (with, say, a written apology to be sent promptly)?

This kind of informed observation clearly needs some preparation. You need to be aware of what should happen, the sequence in which things should be addressed and have a clear idea of how it should all be done.

7. *Analyse what happened afterwards:* this should be done, as has been said, without leading the trainee too much (see comments made earlier in this chapter) and in light of the plan for observation referred to in 6, above.

8. *Link lessons to follow-up action:* at this point you may need to summarise, to refer to written guidelines, or notes may need to be made (by either or both parties) relative to action on future occasions.

9. *Arrange and agree follow-up action and timing:* if you feel there is a need to spend more time on the matter, then a follow-up session may be necessary and should be scheduled for a specific date (otherwise good general intentions can easily be overtaken by events). This may need confirming in writing, especially if it is complex. Perhaps several, staged additional sessions are necessary, perhaps a project of some sort for the trainee is to be specified and required to take place between one session and the next.

10. *End on a note of encouragement:* and link to whatever comes next.

Note: The chain of events that must take place must be tailored to the particular circumstances. This is a fairly typical example; other things may not need to be so complex, others might need a chain of events that runs through several sessions and across a longer period of time (days or weeks).

utilising appropriate methods

Several methods, beyond simple advice and counselling, can routinely be built into on-the-job training, as the following comments show. Beyond these, it can be linked to any other methodology, or combination of methodologies, from the training armoury (many of which are mentioned elsewhere in this book). The main methods include:

■ *Demonstration:* this is important; there is no substitute for seeing. How it is done and who does it will depend on the skill being developed. One thing should always be borne in mind, however: when it is done it must work. This may imply practice (by the manager), careful choice regarding who else undertakes demonstration, or careful selection of a case (as with the example of complaint handling used above). In the latter case, indeed with anything where perfection cannot be guaranteed, a range of examples may produce sufficient going well to establish credibility and make an effective lesson.

The moral for the manager is to exercise care. If you say something like, 'I will show you how, just watch', then your planning and skills must be up to it. That is not, of course, to say that a manager must be expert in everything. After all, 'You don't have to be able to lay eggs to be a chicken farmer', as the old saying has it. But if you say you can, you better deliver if credibility is to be preserved!

■ *Role-play:* this is investigated as a formal technique elsewhere (see page 65); here suffice to say that it has a role as part of explanation, demonstration and particularly in the analysis that follows. If you are trying to prompt a discussion and get someone to float ideas about ways of doing things then, certainly with interactive skills, this technique works well. Often there is a case in mind already. For example, with the topic of complaint handling referred to above, a call is undertaken and observed. That observation shows that there are lessons to be learnt, so role-play might then be used, informally, between you and the trainee. This might only be for a couple of minutes. For instance, you ask how else something could have been done: 'When they said, "I just don't believe you!" what else might you have said? Let me be the customer for a moment, and we'll run the conversation between us.' The lessons this may produce can then be discussed further.

Role-play might need more setting up the first time it is done, and it always needs to be clear to both parties just what is under review and how it will be done, but it can also become routine. If you regularly do this with people they will quickly get the message; especially if they perceive it to be useful.

▓ *Checklists and manuals:* a variety of forms of written material can be used in this context. This is especially useful when you know the session will repeat (through staff turnover, perhaps) and it is worthwhile writing something up. Again, complaint handling is a good example. It may well be that a fair number of people around the organisation need to know how to do this correctly, and material created as part of teaching them so to do will pay for the time it takes.

Such material can be designed with a self-contained quality to it. This might be programmed learning (in text or computer form) that takes trainees through the principles, asks questions and brings them back to reinforce matters where answers are not correct.

Whatever the methodology, on-the-job training is, for many managers, a prime part of the way in which their development responsibilities are implemented.

learning on the job

Another principle worth noting is that of building learning of some sort into activities that would occur in any case. If this can be done, time can be saved. This is certainly possible with many executive skills, as an example will illustrate.

In one company where I undertook training work on presentational skills, they arranged to reinforce formal courses with practice. This is, after all, a skill where practice is essential (however good an initial course). Certain regular meetings were identified and it was made mandatory that any significant contribution that could be anticipated in advance must, for a period, be made formally. The individual had to stand up and was encouraged to use visual aids. In this way the number of presentations they made was artificially increased; and with it the practice they got. Certain 'presentations' could be further designated for subsequent discussion. Preparation also provided an opportunity to seek counselling. All increased the skill that people developed.

It is worth seeking other such opportunities. Little time or planning is necessary, especially if it is originated, as in this case, at the same time as any more formal training input on the same subject.

an economy of scale

One thing that you should avoid is unnecessary repetition. Look for individuals with similar development needs. If James and Julie both need some strengthening in the same way, get them together. This may not only save you time, it may be more fun and interesting for them and more motivational too, each knowing they are not the only one having difficulty.

A further economy of scale comes with matters of reinforcement (or matters new to all) when action can be directed towards improvement at group meetings. In most organisations

teams do get together and meet on a regular basis. Such meetings may be for various reasons, for example to:

- disseminate or exchange information;
- discuss matters, contribute to or make decisions;
- motivate people;
- check progress towards targets and take action to fine-
  tune results;
- spark creativity (as in a brainstorming session).

There can usefully be a development element to the agenda of
staff meetings of this sort. When there is it does not necessarily
need to be labelled 'training', but it does need to be organised.
A manager can use a session at a group meeting for a variety of
purposes, such as to:

- improve the basis of knowledge (of products or procedures, for example);
- introduce new areas of skill not required in the past;
- reinforce existing skills or refine them in the light of
  change;
- practise a technique or skill.

In addition to just achieving whatever is required, such sessions
are an opportunity to get people involved and participating,
and thinking. Some topics may need to be revisited regularly
just to give existing, but important, skills an additional honing.
If this can be done in a way that adds variety – and avoids the
group feeling, 'Oh, no: not that again' – so much the better.

A good way of doing it is to use individuals to hook into a
topic in a new or topical way. The opportunity for this may
arise in one-to-one sessions with individuals. You touch on a
topic, their thinking or their experience is good and you can set
something up for a planned meeting – 'That's interesting, can
you think it through a little more and prepare to speak about
how you reckon this problem can be solved when the group

meets next week? It ought to lead into some useful discussion.' This gives you a way to put ideas over to the group that are not labelled as, 'The manager says do it this way.' You need to give someone due warning and an opportunity to prepare (if you unleash it on them *at* a meeting it may well be resented and the session may go less well). Your team will quickly get used to the fact that you do this, individuals may well be flattered to be asked, so it may be important to share round the lead in such little projects progressively.

Other useful ways of revisiting topics with the group include the use of training films; this is dealt with on page 80. There is also the use of exercises; you may be able to create such things yourself, linked very specifically to current operational matters. Alternatively, much ready-made material can be bought in to act as the foundation of such group activities (see page 63).

The possibilities here are wide-ranging. Exercises and the like can be made a regular, expected and valued feature of such meetings. All that is necessary is some thought beforehand and the time spent can then produce a developmental boost for a whole team of people.

Before moving on to look more broadly at a selection of other development methods in the next chapter, it is worth touching on one special form that is, in essence, a kind of training on the job: mentoring.

mentoring

A mentor is someone who exercises a low-key and informal developmental role. More than one person can be involved in the mentoring of a single individual, and one of them might be the line manager – but more typically in terms of how the word is used, a mentor is specifically *not* the recipient's line manager. It might be someone more senior, on the same level or from elsewhere in the organisation. Often the individual may create the relationship. The finding of mentors and the setting up of mentoring relationships is a useful part of a manager's work in developing his or her 'troops'.

What makes a good mentor? Mentors must have authority (this might mean they are senior, or just that they are capable and confident). They should have suitable knowledge and experience, counselling skills, appropriate clout and a willingness to spend some time with the individual concerned. Finding that time may be a challenge. One way is to organise mentoring on a swap basis: a colleague makes a regular input to one of your team and you do the same for a member of their team.

Then a series of informal meetings can result, together creating a thread through the operational activity. These meetings need an agenda (at least an informal one), but more importantly they need to be constructive. If they are, then one thing will naturally lead to another and a variety of occasions can be utilised to maintain the dialogue. A meeting, followed by a brief encounter as people pass on the stairs; a project, and a promise to spend a moment on feedback; an e-mail or two passing in different directions – all may contribute. What makes this process useful is the commitment and quality of the mentor. Where such relationships can be set up, and where they work well, they add a powerful dimension to the ongoing cycle of development, one that it is difficult to imagine being bettered in any other way.

Overall, what people learn from the ongoing interactions and communications they have with their line manager (and others) can be invaluable. It may leave some matters to be coped with in other ways, but it can prove the best way to cope with many matters and add useful reinforcement in areas of development that also need a more formal approach.

Finally, remember that on-the-job development activity is, when it works well, one of the most important for those people who say, 'I'm motivated by working for a manager from whom I learn.' And most staff do say exactly that – yours are likely to be no exception.

horses for courses

The need for ongoing updating, adding and extension to people's skills and experience has, I believe, been established. But you cannot *make* people change in this way; indeed some of those people falling by the wayside in today's competitive economies are those refusing to adapt. That said, as good a definition as any of development and training is that it is a process of helping people to learn. Certainly as a definition it has the merits of being short and focusing on both sides of the process, recognising that both manager and trainee play a part.

In this chapter we review a variety of developmental methods: ways of providing help in learning. This is both to comment on some of the main methodologies themselves, and also to show that there are a variety of ways in which assistance can be provided. Indeed it is also to show that there is no definitive list of methods, but that part of the manager's job is to seek new ways (or adapt and recombine others) in order to maximise the *opportunity* for development.

The choice of method must blend, and sometimes compromise between, a number of key factors. These include what is most:

■ *effective* (and will be most likely to ensure that learning does take place);

▓ *productive* (and will make the best use of time);

▓ *convenient* (which includes what you are best set up to do, and how much something will disrupt operational matters – or not);

▓ *motivational* (always an important side-effect of development – ideally you must seek to create a positive effect);

▓ *timely* (in the sense of both when the training, or the result of it, is needed and in terms of fitting with other operational considerations of timing);

▓ *fitting* (that is what fits best into the continuum of other, and ongoing, training and development);

▓ *well-tailored* (to the person or group involved, in terms of their job, nature and stage of development);

▓ *financially suitable* (not necessarily the cheapest way of doing something, but it must always be possible to justify the costs).

The choice of method has the overall intention of making the process both effective and productive. Some methods are not mutually exclusive and you may want to do a number of things in combination or in sequence, coming at something from a variety of directions. Smaller examples (can you have a 'small' method?) may act in their own right or be an inherent part of a larger event as, for example, role-playing might be held as a discrete session, or as part of a course.

As has already been said, and as the last chapter evidenced, many ideas and approaches that qualify as methods are extremely simple. That is all to the good, even if they may need some care to get the best from them. It would certainly be wrong to assume more complex forms must predominate: simple ways are useful too. First, however, we review the classic course – something that comes in a surprising variety of guises.

courses, and more courses

There are all sorts of learning events and the terminology is less than exact. There are courses, seminars, meetings, workshops, conferences and more. In considering what to do an assessment has to be made of the options. First, individuals must be selected for training; second, it must be decided just what training is provided; third – our concern here – the question is, which course to select? Answering this is not a science, and judgement and preference play a key part. Some juggling of disparate factors may be necessary, and the following are designed to help cut through the plethora of alternatives and assist some sensible decision making:

- ■ *How long?* Usually this is a compromise between what the content demands, the level of participation and the realism of time away from the job.
- ■ *Internal or external?* Various factors are important here: how many people need training? (A public seminar is ideal for one or two.) Would it be useful to get an outside perspective? To mix with others? What about timing? What internal resources exist?
- ■ *Which trainer?* This involves thinking about who can conduct the programme (ie who has the relevant skills and experience), and who will make it most effective (for example, there may be political overtones to a topic that will be more effectively overcome by an outside trainer with no axe to grind).
- ■ *What format?* Here there are many options, from a short session of a few hours to long courses (see Chapter 7).
- ■ *How much participation?* This is not just a question of what would be most satisfying, but of what the topic needs, the number of participants, etc.
- ■ *The devil you know.* All things being equal, it may make sense to stick with a trainer you have used in the past, and therefore know, to save time in briefing, etc.

There is another factor, always important: *cost*. While poor training may be worse than none at all, one has to be realistic and cost is a factor that dictates, at least in part, what decision is made.

getting the best from course attendance

Whatever course is selected, matters must be arranged so that participants get the best from it. Two factors are important here.

Pre-course briefing: participants should ideally be involved in the choice to attend a particular course, but whether the request comes from them or from a manager they should be clear why they are attending and what should come from it. It is well worth the few minutes it takes to sit down with someone you are sending on a course to go through this. They should be clear what the objectives of a course are, and its limitations – it may only address part of something they ultimately want to deal with comprehensively. They should be encouraged to go with clear and specific personal objectives in mind. Such briefing and thinking sets up attendance so that its effectiveness is maximised.

Behaviour on the programme: training is sufficiently well regarded these days that disruptive and unconstructive participants are rare. Even if someone approaches a course positively, however, they need to maximise the benefit of their attendance on it. After all, once it is over any action may be more difficult and, certainly on a short course, attention to the actual process of attending is worthwhile.

As an example, the boxed material that follows is a set of guidelines given to people attending public courses; it could be issued to delegates at the start of a course or ahead of attendance. It certainly addresses some of the key issues and sets the scene for everyone getting the most from the experience of attending. You could easily prepare an individual version of this sort of thing; and perhaps should do so.

notes for delegates

1. This manual contains all the basic details of this training programme. Further papers will be distributed progressively during the course so that a complete record will be available by the last session.

2. This is *your* seminar, and represents a chance to say what you think – so please do say it. Everyone can learn from the comments of others and the discussion it prompts.

3. Exchange of experience is as valuable as the formal lectures – but you need to *listen carefully* and try to understand other points of view if this is to work.

4. Do support your views with facts in discussion, use examples and stick to the point.

5. Keep questions and comments succinct – do not monopolise the proceedings, but let others have a say so that various viewpoints can be discussed.

6. Make points in context as they arise. Remember that participation is an attitude of mind. It includes listening as well as speaking, but also certainly includes constructive disagreement where appropriate.

7. Make notes as the meeting progresses. There is notepaper provided in this binder. Formal notes will provide an aide memoir of the content and coverage, so any additional notes should primarily link to your job and to action on your return to work. Even a few action points noted per session can act as a catalyst and help ensure action follows attendance.

8. A meeting with colleagues, staff or your manager on your return to normal working can be valuable; it acts as a bridge between ideas discussed here and action in the workplace and can make change more likely.

9. It will help everyone present if you wear your name badge, respect the timetable and keep mobile telephones and pagers switched off during the sessions. *

10. This is an opportunity to step back from day-to-day operations and consider issues that can help make your job more effective. Be sceptical of your own operation, challenge ideas, remain open minded throughout and actively seek new thinking that can help you prompt change and improve performance.

Note: this is a good place to list any 'house rules', the observance of which can improve the course experience for everyone attending.

the manager as trainer

Some courses can be home-grown – you can conduct them. Now, you might take the view that you have more than sufficient to do without conducting training sessions. Such a view might be reinforced in light of the time that needs to be spent on informal development. Equally you might say that you are no trainer, and regard anything that needs to be done as much better done by someone else. Perhaps. But there can be occasions when it may be worth re-examining these views and for two reasons.

First, it may sometimes be the only way of achieving something. This would be so, for instance, if:

■ there is no budget;
■ the only resource available (an internal trainer perhaps) does not have the relevant experience for the topic you need or where gaining it would involve prohibitive preparation time;
■ the session must ideally be incorporated into something else such as a departmental or team meeting;
■ outside resources are too far afield or will tie up too much time.

By the same token, there are advantages. Examples include:

- the team working together (without an external party such as a trainer);
- the training content needing to be linked very closely to operational matters (perhaps where your passing on details to a trainer would be a lengthy process);
- when complete control (or confidentiality) is necessary;
- when a series of short inputs (or participative sessions) needs to be programmed into the working schedule and involving another person would be complicated.

There are many examples of training that can usefully be bound up with sessions to do other, operational, things where just having the team together makes good sense. One example that comes to mind is that of developing business writing skills. Here a how-to session about writing effectively can easily – and usefully – incorporate an exercise that works at something real. It might act as a drafting session for a necessary report, perhaps, or create a series of standard documents such as letters to customers. In this way you can kill two birds with one stone.

So, maybe you do need to acquire some basic training skills. This is beyond the brief for this book (however, see my book, *Running an Effective Training Session*, published by Gower). Many managers do come to do some training so I am only advocating what some people make work well. There is no need to do everything yourself, either. If you do plan to conduct a session, there are a number of ways to make doing so easier and quicker than just starting with a blank piece of paper. For example:

- Talk to the HR department or an internal trainer (it will take them less time to help you than to do it all, so they may well be receptive).

▓ Talk to an outside consultant. I have often been asked to develop a course but not to conduct it, or certainly not more than once where a number of repeats are necessary. Typically, either the course is developed and run for an initial group, including the manager, with the manager then able to conduct the repeats. Or the course is developed and all that is run is a briefing session designed to put the manager in a position where he or she can then conduct the programmes thereafter. Suitable materials can assist this process, with slides being designed, and manuals, examples and exercises all laid out in a way that acts to minimise the manager's preparation time.

▓ Use published training exercises (or complete courses). There is a wealth of such material published, not least by the publishers of this book, Kogan Page. Gower, mentioned earlier, also specialises in this field. There are more; all provide things in 'ready to go' formats, often with non-copyright materials (résumé notes can simply be copied and distributed), slides, etc. Costs make this a very economic approach. Even if things are not used slavishly but adapted a little to create the required focus (and this is often the case), they are a useful resource.

The benefits of a manager working closely with a team in this way are many. If you want your people's performance to be excellent, then it pays to be involved with them in its development. This is a manifestation of the old adage about leading from the front. Doing some training, beyond the on-the-job type described earlier, is a useful extension of this sort of involvement. You can start slowly – a short session or participative exercise at the next departmental meeting, perhaps. Get some assistance organised initially by all means, but give it a go. You might be surprised just how quickly it becomes an aspect of your management style; one that is useful and of which your staff approve.

The next section looks at a technique which, as well as being a part of what is used during courses, is exactly the sort of thing an individual manager can use informally. This idea was raised earlier in looking at on-the-job training. Next we investigate some of the details.

role-play methods

For the manager, an appreciation of role-play as a training technique is useful in two ways. First, simply to be aware of what may be done on courses that your people attend, or indeed to specify that it should be included, for instance when arranging an in-company programme. Second, it is, as has been said, a technique that can be used by any manager in a short session, a departmental meeting where part of the activity is training, or on a one-to-one basis.

The usefulness of role-play is that it provides an opportunity to explore, practise and experiment with skills used in communications in a *safe* environment. For example, in role-play related to customer care skills, there are no real customers to be upset; related to interview techniques there are no real candidates to be inconvenienced. For convenience the comments that follow divide the technique into less and more formal usage.

informal role-play

At its simplest role-play is no more than a momentary enactment of real-life situations. Imagine you are concerned to develop interview skills of some sort with a member of your staff. You can set up a scenario in a moment: 'Imagine that the applicant says… . What would you reply?', and let this lead on to a conversation (with either party taking either role) in which the situation is explored, the conversation continued and the way in which points are made are exemplified.

This conversation – the role-play – can then be the basis of discussion and debate. Subsequent discussion would focus on analysis of what happened. Was the response a good one? Did it achieve what it set out to do? If not, how else might something have been put? And so on. You can extend the point of view and questions raised by swapping the roles people play.

It is obviously sensible to have clear objectives, so that both parties understand what element of the communication they are trying to represent and what its purpose is. This, coupled with the training objectives, puts the whole thing in context. Simply pushing someone into a role-play conversation will achieve little. Tell them the topic under review, describe how role-play works and define exactly the characters and situation you suggest addressing, and it can become a valuable tool.

This can be done one-to-one or in a meeting: picking participants to produce an example or giving everyone a turn if time permits. Regular use quickly persuades people of its usefulness and negates the need to explain the principles involved again and again. At this stage it is a quick and straightforward thing to do as well as a useful one.

formal role-play

Formal role-play is most often an inherent part of a training session or course. It may involve not just doing what is described above in a more formal way and in a more formal environment, but more sophisticated methods also. This normally means using audio or video equipment to record the role-play so that replaying it can form the basis of more detailed critique designed to lead to change.

Although this is a tried-and-tested technique and there is no reason for it not to work well, it does need some care. Certainly there are things that can jeopardise its success. Potential dangers include:

- ▓ over-awareness of the camera;
- ▓ overacting to the camera, indeed a belief that role-play demands 'acting';
- ▓ the difficulty of being 'on show' in front of peers;
- ▓ poor role-play briefs;
- ▓ incomplete or unconstructive feedback after the role-play is complete;
- ▓ those watching feeling excluded.

More positively, role-play can be organised to avoid the above and to achieve one or more of the following:

- ▓ reproduce real life as closely as possible;
- ▓ allow practice of important, difficult or unusual situations;
- ▓ introduce and practise a skill new to people;
- ▓ develop confidence;
- ▓ experiment with new approaches;
- ▓ change negative habits or reinforce positive ones;
- ▓ reinforce knowledge and instil useful reflexes;
- ▓ utilise analytical skills (used in the feedback and critique).

The classic role-play is most often used to focus on interactive skills. It should be approached – systematically – in way that is well considered and focused on the objectives. Below is a typical example. While nothing of this nature should be slavishly followed, it nonetheless offers useful guidelines for successful role-playing.

---

classic role-play: a formula

The following sets out the key stages:

1. Explain or issue (they may be in writing) the briefs concerning the chosen scenario to the two participants

and allow them time to plan how they will work. If either is literally playing themselves this should be clear. Note, too, that participants using other than their own names quickly risks confusion.

2. State the objectives and summarise the briefs, adding any background detail that is important, for the rest of the group.

3. Allocate any general or specific observation tasks to other members of the group; it may work best if everyone has something to do.

4. Unless you are doing it yourself, brief the video camera operator (for instance, explaining whether the contribution of one person is to be captured on film, or both).

5. Deal with timing (for example, instruct people to stop after 10 minutes or at a particular point in the conversation).

6. Invite questions, to be sure everyone is clear.

7. Always make it clear that the exercise is to create an example for discussion and is a group exercise (although it can provide individual feedback too). It may be worth saying here that it should be made clear that any tape recordings will be destroyed after the session, as the thought that they won't can make people play safe, and their experimenting may not be what is required.

8. Set the role-play off.

9. Keep notes of when and where in what transpires you wish to comment, prompt discussion or ask questions (these can usefully be linked to the counter on the recorder).

10. When the session ends:
    - Thank everyone taking part (especially if there was any reticence about it).
    - Ask for initial comments: it is often best to let the participants speak first, but others, observers and yourself, may need to be involved too – albeit briefly at this stage.

- Play back the recording. This can be done in bite-sized segments, with all able to request a stop to make a comment, though this session must be chaired firmly.
- Ensure that feedback is constructive and that the emphasis is positive. Of course, some negative comment may be appropriate, but the final need is a positive link to next time and to real situations.
- Following discussion, segments of the video might be shown again to highlight key points.
- Summarise, so that key – and positive – points are the last memory of the session. Such final words should highlight the general points, applicable to the entire group, rather than the individual.

This kind of approach can be repeated as appropriate during a longer training session.

For formal sessions, or topics that you need to return to, it may be worth devising a checklist/feedback form to facilitate the group focusing on key issues.

Other forms of role-play are possible and a brief word follows about three useful ones:

▨ *Carousel role-play:* this takes the role-play around a group and is a quick way of involving everyone. The scenario is set up; then the first two participants (perhaps in line around a U-shaped meeting room) begin the conversation. After a few minutes, at a convenient point, the manager will stop the conversation and ask the next two in line to continue. This can be repeated a number of times until the conversation reaches a conclusion or everyone has had a turn; better still, both. Everyone has to listen carefully as the conversation must really *continue*: what the first participants said must be reflected in the following segments of the role-play. It can be analysed as before and may, or may not, be recorded.

■ *Silent role-play:* here the role-play format is followed, but what people believe should be said is *written down*. There is no talking, and each 'statement' is preceded by the reading of what was said last by the next to 'speak'. This can only be used for short sessions, but is useful when the detail and degree of precision of what is said is important (eg describing procedures to customers where the explanation must be 100 per cent clear and put over fast). Again analysis can follow and comment can be made on *exactly* the phraseology used.

■ *Triad role-play:* this refers to interactive situations involving three rather than two people (or more, though care should be taken: complication can easily escalate and negate any positive effect). Sometimes this is necessary if real life is to be portrayed accurately, for example many job appraisal meetings involve three people and if such meetings are to be explored using role-play a third person must be involved. Provided as ever the brief is clear, this can work perfectly well.

Now, back to courses – and another type to consider.

activity courses

One special form of course is worth a mention. Imagine: it is cold and wet, moorland stretches away into the mist and you know the nearest cup of tea and warm bath are miles distant. You and assorted colleagues are huddled under the dripping branches of a tree. On the ground nearby are three old car tyres, some lengths of rope, six planks of wood and a cushion. How do you turn all that into something that floats, cross the river and... where actually is the river? The 'outward bound' type of course is loved and hated in equal measure.

Some people swear they are the ultimate developer of leadership skills or teamwork. Some just swear. Certainly their use needs care. Not every provider of such things is equally good; some are good at providing a physical challenge, but less good at relating it in any meaningful way to the workplace. Not every group is suited to this sort of thing, and certainly someone less physically able or adept might find tagging along after their more athletic team mates taught them nothing but resentment.

That said, activity courses seem to suit the culture of some organisations and, if they do, they provide a different way of approaching certain training tasks. They are almost certain to get the undivided attention of the group for a while; it is pretty difficult to worry about immediate operational problems when you are high in the air dangling on the end of a rope over mud of indeterminate depth.

The decision process about signing up to a course is similar to that already described. You have to weigh up a number of factors and see what makes best sense. First and foremost you need to consider whether this kind of training should take a slice of your training budget, then find the right course if the answer is that it should (bearing in mind that safety is a factor here, given that the classroom may be more like half a county).

It may be that on occasion the element of fun that many find in such programmes should win out over more formal, classroom style training. If it fits then by all means use it, but do not let the fun element submerge whatever more serious training objectives you have. As with anything else, you will get most from the investment if you set clear objectives and communicate them to participants.

simulations

Almost at the other end of the spectrum of training methods from activity courses, simulations focus attention very specifically on one area of activity. The teaching is through involvement, often with technology lending a hand. Typically a computer program provides the basis to experiment with complex interactions.

For example, there are simulations used in marketing training. They set up a market situation: products, prices, people, markets, competitors and more. Decision making can be input and not only recorded, but also recorded in such a way that the whole complex web of 'given' factors changes. Thus a decision to raise a product's price will see volume sold and profitability adjust accordingly, and competitors' action taken in response. Some such training devices are for individuals to use, others work – sometimes competitively – with a group of people participating together.

They can provide considerable realism and stimulation. They tend not to be suitable as a first exposure to a topic, relying as they do on the participants having some knowledge of the subject. They need clear briefing and sometimes preparatory work to set them up, but this is understandable given their role and purpose.

If you want to check out this sort of thing, a good example is a marketing training device called *Markstrat*. The organisation producing this, and it is one that has been around a while and is tried and tested, is StratX Ltd (based in Beaconsfield, tel: 01494 680700); if you check their Web site it will give you a flavour of how it all works (www.stratx.com).

management games

There are also a variety of management games in much simpler formats. Again these are things you can buy ready-made from a variety of providers (an example is the company Training Essentials, tel: 016974 72100). Many of the 'kits' comprise items to be used in some kind of team game – simple components such as shapes, building devices (bricks, rods or whatever). They create a team exercise that can be slotted into a training event, or used on its own at a team or departmental meeting. While they are, for the most part, self-contained – everything is there including the instructions – many can be made to work best when facilitated by someone with a degree of training experience.

They can be fun, have a significant positive effect on learning and are worth a try. It is useful to check carefully the level of prior training experience that is needed to use one, and how well they fit with your training circumstances and objectives. And it is always worth preparing very carefully: read the instructions, check the components, even try it out on your children – but make absolutely sure that you are 100 per cent sure you have it all worked out before you try to instruct others how to go about it.

Simpler, home-grown versions are also good value. Most trainers have their favourite. My own involves two jigsaw puzzles that a group needs to complete simultaneously. I have especially fond memories of one course on which I used this, and of the normally very upright director in charge of the group of managers involved standing on the table urging his team on, well, let us say with a vengeance. It should be noted here that if such an exercise is designed to enhance, say, communications or decision-making skills in some way, then the 'trainer' needs expertise in the relevant topic.

Such formal means of extending and giving purpose to participation on courses and training events are worth experimenting with and bearing in mind for the future.

packaged training

This term is usually used to describe training resources with two characteristics. First, they use a variety of aids including audio and video material, programmed learning texts and, of course, computer-based training, particularly using

CD ROMs. Second, they are designed to work on a sometimes largely unsupervised solo basis or, if with a group, through 'facilitation' (someone to lead the way through, rather than a fully-fledged trainer).

The simplest form will set participants off down a road involving a number of elements. They work through a workbook. They pause on occasion as they do so: to view video clips, listen to audio elements, answer questions (which with programmed learning devices can redirect them, recapping if knowledge is not proven to be at a certain level) or, where group work is involved, to interact with others.

The greatest advantages of packaged training are perhaps twofold. *With large numbers of trainees:* once a kit is created or purchased it is available as a permanent resource. Any number of people can be put through it and this, assuming it works well in a particular situation, can save a great deal of time and is likely to be highly cost-effective in the long term.

With topics linked to straightforward processes: in other words where the matter can be learnt almost by rote. This is true, for instance, of certain physical actions (some of the large motor companies teach engineers how to service their cars through this method). Where there is a judgemental element to the topic, this must be addressed through exercises or examples (eg videoed case histories), or even through some other training mechanism entirely. This may not be a good way to train in interactive skills such as negotiation, for example.

Again there is a plethora of available material, but this really needs to be seen and exhibitions provide a good way of checking a number of options in one place. Another option, given sufficient importance, budget and number of trainees, may be to create your own.

A final point worth making here concerns timing. This sort of training device may take only a little time to go through and a schedule can be set up that minimises the effect on normal operations. Maybe packages can be used over a lunchtime, or a series of lunchtimes (with free sandwiches provided as a small incentive, perhaps), or at the end of the day after normal work concludes.

brainstorming

This may not immediately seem to be a training technique. But it does have training ramifications. Many managers bemoan how uncreative their people are, yet are uncertain how to prompt them to be otherwise. Brainstorming not only formalises the process of creativity, it can have an effect outside the specific sessions involved – it alerts people to the possibilities and shows them how to be more creative (and if it does that then it is helping them to learn). As such it is a good example of using techniques, valuable in their own right, to swell the overall weight of training and development in the widest sense. Doing so makes good, and productive, sense.

Some brief guidelines for successful brainstorming are given in the boxed section below.

---

brainstorming: guidelines for success

Brainstorming is a group activity and can be used to provide an almost instant burst of idea generation. Working with a group of people (maybe three or four works most easily but up to a dozen is manageable) it needs a prescribed approach, thus:

- ▨ Gather people around and explain the objectives (what exactly you are seeking ideas about and why).
- ▨ Explain that there are to be *no comments* on ideas at this stage.
- ▨ Allow a little time for thought (singly or, say, in pairs).
- ▨ Start taking contributions and noting them down (publicly on a flipchart or similar).

- ■ When a good-sized list is established and recorded, analysis can begin.
- ■ Grouping similar ideas together can make the list more manageable.
- ■ Open-minded discussion can then review the list.
- ■ Identify ideas that can be taken forward.

Such a session must exclude the word 'impossible' from the conversation, at least initially (and especially when used in senses such as, 'It's impossible, we don't do things that way' (why not?) or 'It's impossible, we tried it once and it didn't work' (how long ago and in what form?)

By avoiding any negative or censorious first responses, by allowing one idea to spark another and variations on a theme to refine a point (perhaps taking it from something wild to something practical), a brainstorming session can produce genuinely new approaches.

It can be fun to do, satisfying in outcome and time-efficient to undertake – and a group that brainstorms regularly gets better at it, and quicker and more certain in its production of good, useable, ideas. Try it – you might be surprised at the results.

development circles

Some years ago the Japanese were using a technique, taken up around the world in various ways, called 'quality circles'. The idea was that a continuous focus could be kept on quality (primarily in a factory and production context) and a flow of ideas generated, the best of which could be taken up, implemented and used to yield productivity increases. Circles, groups of people of a size to facilitate discussion, were set up. Over time they looked at a whole series of issues (eg something specific such as reducing waste of raw materials in a particular phase of production) and essentially brainstormed the matter.

Ideas were fed up the organisation, through a hierarchy of groups, the best and most practical being approved by management and coordinated into operations. Communication was organised to be two-way so that everyone knew what was being achieved.

The basic principle of a permanent, or semi-permanent, organisation of people focused on improvements has been copied and modified and made to work usefully in many different contexts since the idea of quality circles originated. An area in which a similar approach has been used is that of customer service.

This sort of procedure can, like brainstorming on its own, produce learning in the area of creativity. Arranged with this sort of formality it can also direct people towards a whole range of other useful skills. Someone has to chair the sessions, people have to listen and contribute. Matters have to be reported back up the line, reports have to be written and presentations made. An element of competition and incentive has often been used to add to people's concentration (a bonus payment for the team producing the most valuable idea, perhaps).

Thus, such a scheme can be used overtly or otherwise to progress a variety of development aims with some of these skills in mind. It is a good example of development and operational activity being progressed usefully alongside each other so that both gain.

open learning

This phrase is used to encapsulate a number of techniques linking work done 'at your desk' to a central point elsewhere that coordinates the activity (hence the alternative name, 'distance learning'). This has become a popular way of handling the load of studying for some sort of qualification, where exercises, projects and such like are set and marked by tutors at the body offering the course. Study may involve all sorts of mixtures of method, from reading to watching videos provided and, of course, computer work (some now online).

The principle is also used for job-based training and an open learning set-up may exist in a large organisation where staff work in many widely spread locations.

resource centres

These are often the preserve of larger companies. The idea developed from the simple library and that element remains. Beyond that, however, the resource centre has a range of developmental materials and the equipment these demand. Here someone can go and watch a video, spend time at a dedicated computer learning station (see the boxed section below), engage in certain small-group activities – or just find a helpful book.

There is no one definition of a resource centre. Different organisations configure them differently, and of course they change over time. Not only do they provide an aid to learning, their very existence contributes to the creation of a development culture, demonstrates that development is important and helps both managers and staff fit undertaking development into a busy life.

keeping up with technology

The permutations of technology used for training change as you watch. Trainers and training sessions apart, it is possible to use audio- and video-based training, and even here there are variations. In considering options always check what the 'lead' element is. For example, do participants watch a video that tells them to turn to a workbook for a spell? Or do they read something, a manual for instance, which tells them to watch a video clip (or listen to audio material) periodically as they proceed through the written material?

Things that are described as free-standing often leave something to be desired and it can dilute training effectiveness simply to use material with not even an introduction to position it in the context of the operational situation of participants. Objectives vary too. Some training is designed to convey a detailed knowledge of something, in other cases it is primarily designed to prompt discussion, thinking or practice. Always be clear what you are using.

Beyond simple elements like audio and video there is a variety of computer-based devices. CD ROMs provide a degree of interactive experience and lend themselves to recapping and to checking knowledge gained at particular points. Most organisations have the equipment necessary to use them.

It is impossible here to list comprehensively the various formats available. Suffice to say that when a suitable technology appears someone will produce training that uses it. So courses exist in open-learning form, online, on DVD and more. However good the technology, its effectiveness is still dependent on the content. Interesting things are happening. By all means keep up to date, explore new formats and test new methods, but match whatever you use to the needs and do not use technology as an easy option – *plug in and train*. One of the roles of the Training Manager is to keep up to date on such things. Keep in touch (maybe they want people to try things out on) and you can keep up to date without scouring the market, or the Internet, every five minutes.

job rotation and swapping

There are a variety of ways to incorporate development into the everyday work of the organisation. Sometimes this is simply a matter of change. People are intentionally moved into new jobs, rather different to what they were doing previously, for developmental reasons, and there is a domino effect as people move round. I deal with some organisations where this is an established pattern: no one expects to stay in the same post for more than a few years. Not only is this seen as aiding the development of the individuals concerned, it is regarded as stimulating the new thinking and new ideas necessary to prevent the organisation becoming struck in a rut. It also may benefit staff retention (people are less likely to leave through boredom).

ready for anything

Other methods include secondments (dealt with in Chapter 7), the use of training films (see the end of this chapter), and more. A complete list of methods is neither possible nor intended. Indeed the inventive manager or trainer will keep adding to any list they do have as time goes by.

It is worth putting yourself in a position to check, quickly and regularly, what is being made available in the area of training methods and resources. Thus is may be worthwhile to:

- subscribe to various training journals;
- subscribe also to relevant newsletters and e-zines delivered automatically to your computer;
- allow your name to be added to certain mailing lists (for instance to get news of the latest products from a training film company);
- occasionally (regularly?) attend one of the big training exhibitions;
- cultivate a friend in the Human Resources department (or similar) especially if you are in a large organisation;
- undertake a little networking so that your own experience of development activity is extended by learning what others do.

The next chapter looks at more methods, this time from a longer-term perspective. But first – more about films.

using training films

Curiously, perhaps, in an age of video, CD ROMs and who knows what else, people tend still to talk simply about 'training films'. Certainly there is a profusion of these available, for purchase or rental, and typically consisting of 20–40 minutes' worth of material. They do represent a useful option – a way of providing, or augmenting, training without elaborate preparation.

They should not, however, be regarded as an easy option: just drag people together, stick on a film and say, 'Look and listen.' So, how do you get the most from training films?

selecting the right film

Let us assume that the topic is decided. You know that you want people to develop a certain skill and want to find a film on that subject. There are not that many providers and it does not take long to check catalogues and Web sites or make a telephone call to check what is available. If there is a film that seems suitable, you will want to be able to assess it – is it any good? – is it suitable for *your people*? Consider:

■ *The provider:* to some degree the standard (and style) of what you will get can be gauged by the company producing or distributing the film. Although even films from the big, well-known operators may vary a little in standard, this is a good first measure.

■ *The film quality:* given the standard of what people are used to seeing in the cinema and on television, a minimum standard is probably necessary. However, this is not to say that simpler things cannot be useful; one of my own 'most-used' films consists of live action, real people filmed doing real things, with no script or expensive production values – but it makes some good, clear points and is a valuable training resource.

■ *The message:* how the film puts over its message is vital. If it tries to do too much in a short time, for instance, it may not succeed. If it allows humour to submerge the message, this too may dilute its effectiveness. Not least, does its style match your circumstances? Will your people be able to identify with the characters and circumstances in the film? Does the message match the kind of way the topic needs to be dealt with in your organisation?

You can get some advice from catalogues or recommendations from colleagues, but there is no substitute for seeing for yourself. Most providers have systems for previewing that work well and the time this takes, and even the small cost sometimes involved, is worthwhile. You need to plan to use not just a film, but a suitable film.

using the film

The first thing to note is that using a training film is not an opportunity to train without effort. Most films are not designed to do a complete job unsupported. At the very least they need topping and tailing; more often they are most effective when incorporated into a session, albeit sometimes a short one.

Usually a film is supplied with training notes, a booklet or guide to its use. These should always be studied. They do not need to be followed slavishly: their suggestions for sessions can be changed, lengthened, shortened or otherwise amended. But they can be useful. For example, they may help clarify exactly why a film is being used – the role it will play. This can vary. It may be to:

- introduce a topic;
- summarise key issues;
- crack through the core content, the essential principles of something;
- spark discussion;
- link to a particular internal situation.

Whatever you do it must be clear. The film should help you meet your training objectives and it should be evident how it will do so and what role it will play (and this also needs to be made clear to the group). You can plan film use specifically and systematically following something like this sequence:

- Always watch the film through yourself ahead of the session.
- Read the accompanying material.
- Make notes of anything you need to mention, emphasise or explain to the group.
- Decide how the training points made in the film link to the totality of what you want to achieve.
- List ways in which the film can link to participation or exercises, noting questions that the group should address.
- Link your thinking into your overall preparation of the whole session.

It is worth thinking just a little about the physical use of a film. Set things up so that everyone can see. You may want to dim the lights, but not too much if people have to make notes. Remember that some films are designed to be seen in several parts, or have a separate summary section that allows you to return to key points at the end of a session. *Note:* certain films are designed in a way that links to individual study (particularly those available on CD ROM). While introduction and briefing may still be necessary, subsequent solo study may sometimes work well from a time standpoint, for example allowing individual members of a department to see the film without the operational disruption of a group session.

The style of the film will allow different forms of training to stem from it. For instance:

▓ Case-study-based films allow one form of discussion, for example extending the scenario or varying elements of it in discussion – 'What would have happened if that had not been the reaction when...?'

▓ Behaviourally based films may allow more analysis of how people react, or even allow links to be made to real people in your own company.

▓ The classic wrong way/right way film style in which characters perform badly (exhibiting the dangers), learn lessons and then perform better (exhibiting the strengths of using correct technique), allow both aspects to be reviewed or discussed.

stop/start use

As an example of stop/start use, let's consider the good way/bad way film. By showing the film in parts, starting with the 'bad way', it can be alternated with discussion, asking:

▓ What went wrong and why?
▓ How could matters have been handled differently?
▓ What are the principles involved to ensure success?

Then the 'right way' part can be shown and separate discussion can follow. Role-play could be organised to extrapolate the situations portrayed in the film with members of the group extending the film characters' roles.

humour in films

Many films use humour to create the style of a film. UK producing company Video Arts pioneered this approach (actor John Cleese was among its founders), and most of its films are humorous. Paraphrasing what I have seen of their views of this, they say that: humour overcomes any resentment or prejudice about being trained, making it seem non-threatening and acceptable (this is particularly true of more experienced staff, who can see the film as 'a bit of fun' rather than something 'they need'). Humour makes the training message more memorable, providing an additional set of memories – the funny bits – and, from them, prompts to the learning points.

Anything that helps training lessons stick is all to the good; the only danger is the occasional film where the humour is overdone and the message is lost or diluted rather than enhanced.

A key overall advantage of using films on occasion is simply one of variety. Showing a film rings the changes, varies the pace and makes a break from lectures or other forms of participation. It perhaps injects some humour and sparks off a whole range of additional activity. Films are no panacea, and their use needs consideration, organisation and planning – they are not a crutch allowing managers to abrogate their personal responsibility for what goes on in a training session – but they are useful.

home grown

Making a film internally is a major undertaking. It demands experience, expertise and often a substantial budget. It is possible, however, to create your own filmed material in a simple form and yet which is a real asset. This can be done with professional help (a consultant, a video producer), or can be tried just by pointing a camera at something – even if the something may need a bit of organising!

The details of exactly how this sort of thing could be done, certainly in film production terms, are somewhat beyond our brief here. However, two examples with which I was involved in the past show the span of possibilities.

Role-play. With careful planning (and maybe a little luck) role-play examples can hit a standard that makes them of lasting value. With two consultant colleagues, I once helped produce a two-part video showing something of the right and wrong ways to negotiate. While consisting of little more than talking heads, and utilising no sophisticated film-making expertise, the carefully planned role-play produced excellent lessons and made the film worthy of use beyond its original purpose.

Real life. With the brief of keeping costs low yet producing a real and effective training resource, I once produced a film for a trade association. It focused on aspects of sales technique, and the characters filmed were real: one of the sales team from a member company and a real client. Their permission and cooperation were obtained (this included their providing the location), and with some briefing a real meeting was filmed literally as it happened. With minimal editing and some added commentary (and an accompanying workbook) it became as useful as many more professionally made films – and had the merit of reflecting the exact situation of the kind of business involved.

There are approaches here that may stand experiment. But when one telephone call can put a professionally made film on your desk for a small rental charge, this remains the easiest route when you have decided to use a film for training and development.

long-term training

There was a time when long bouts of training were common, certainly for those people in the middle and higher reaches of an organisation. People saw it as a distinct possibility, and looked forward to their secretary responding to enquiries as to their whereabouts by saying something like, 'He's away for six months; in Cambridge, Massachusetts' (the location of Harvard Business School). Currently the whole environment in which organisations exist seems increasingly pressurised. Staff numbers and other resources may be lower than in the past, yet demands for results are often higher. There is also a greater degree of uncertainty in organisational life. The classic 'jobs for life' tag put on some careers is largely a thing of the past, and stress and pressure may be the order of the day.

One result of all this, tacitly already mentioned here, is that it is more difficult to make time for things that are important in face of an apparently endless list of things that are, or seem, urgent. Certainly as a training consultant I am regularly asked, and sometimes told, to keep the duration of training down to one, two or some short number of days. And I recently found myself at cross-purposes with one prospective client, with me mistakenly thinking they were talking about a one-day session, when it suddenly become apparent that they were looking for two and a half hours over lunchtime! Some training is doubtless better than none, and given oranges, as they say, the job is to make marmalade. So short sessions – however defined – will certainly occur and must be made useful.

Given some probable shortage of time, current circumstances may not be ideal in some organisations to consider development of long duration. There are some organisations, too, in which you would not want to be away for long. If you did go away for six months, you would be likely to return to find that your job had changed (or gone) or that the organisation itself had changed its name, activity or moved away. I exaggerate – I think.

Even so there is merit in a chapter with the words 'long' and 'term' in the title, and a number of useful areas to consider.

long courses

First, a brief word about courses that are simply long. How you define this will depend on the topic and the level of individual who might attend. While it is common enough for people to attend two- or three-day seminars, two or three months or more (which goes beyond what was reviewed in Chapter 5) is much less the norm.

The criteria here are surely similar to the selection of any training (see page 58). The added considerations are assessing the likely benefit of a larger than usual cost, and the difficulty of a longer than usual period without someone 'in post'.

It is important that the real criteria are assessed. Some people will see the desirability of the experience of, say, spending three months in some attractive business school, perhaps in a foreign city, in very personal terms. So, too, with some extensive product training in the factory on the other side of the world. It is only natural. But a considered judgement is necessary. Given that, attendance for some on longer programmes can certainly be valuable.

There may also be training necessary in topics that, by their nature, demand a long training exposure to achieve whatever is desired. A good example of this is language training. Many companies with staff posted in foreign locations need to have them 'immersed' in the local language. Senior people might spend an hour every morning in one-to-one tuition, with this continuing for weeks or months. Nothing less may do the job: *zut alors*!

well qualified

The usefulness of qualifications varies. They can be overrated (it was said at one time, for instance, that the most profitable business to be in was to trade in MBAs: buying them for what they were worth, and selling them for what others *thought* they were to be worth! Sorry, I digress). But there is inherent merit in the principle. There is also a veritable profusion of publications. Certainly reviewing them all is beyond the scope of this short publication.

In order to comment on this area constructively it is convenient to divide qualifications into two broad camps. First, there are those that are a must, in the sense that they are a requirement for a particular job; for instance, you cannot be a Chartered Accountant without passing the relevant exams (some years' worth, in fact). In addition, many jobs specify qualifications as a prerequisite for candidates who wish to be considered. Second, there are those qualifications that are desirable.

Initial qualifications are those that people have when they take up jobs, so here we will concentrate on those qualifications that might be acquired along the way, as it were. There are several reasons that make study for and, all being well, the award of qualifications relevant. Four are mentioned below:

■ *Knowledge acquisition:* this is a most obvious benefit, whether we are talking about an NVQ or a postgraduate degree or something in between. The study involved may provide knowledge that is of immediate or later relevance to the job and the work that it entails.

■ *Accelerated experience:* this is meant in a sense that differs from a straightforward familiarity with a body of knowledge. An example will clarify: attendance on a management course, for instance, may give experience of a whole range of processes. These might include problem solving and decision making, working as a team, being creative, project management, report writing and more. The very nature of the more participative courses may give this experience, and be reinforced by the duration involved.

■ *Changed profile:* a heightened profile may of course benefit the individual, but may have immediate effects of a corporate nature too. In one UK company which was taken over by a Dutch company, the UK accountant had recently added to his qualifications (originally somewhat basic) and was only accepted by the Dutch – who are much more formal about matters of accounting than the British – because of the credibility his list of qualifications now provided. The result was that no one from Holland was imported into a financial role, and the UK staff were able to continue to work with someone in the key financial role whose methods were liked and trusted.

■ *Contact making:* this may be of less importance, indeed is more of a side-effect, but could still be useful. Mingling with a new external group might well yield links and liaisons that, developed by future networking, prove to have positive benefits.

Of course, the form involved can vary almost as much as the topics and qualifications themselves, so much so that it is hardly worth listing more than a few here just to give a flavour of what is possible. They may be full-time, part-time, involve so-called day release (they are part-time, but some of that is in classic working time), or they may involve only evenings. They may involve part of the work being done overseas, working in a second language, or both. Clearly the ways in which study interacts with work and how it affects it differs from one to another.

An organisation, or its HR department, should perhaps have some policy with regard to this kind of development activity.

policy on qualifications

What happens if someone volunteers for this sort of long-term study? An immediate boss may react in isolation, and perhaps on the spur of the moment: 'Sure, you sign up for it, I can put up with losing a few hours a week. It will be very worthwhile – hey, I think we could even get away with charging the tuition fees to our training budget, would that help?'

Costs and time are involved. A further consideration is that people talk. If someone else, in another department and perhaps wanting to do something wholly different, is offered less than their colleague they will want to know the reason why. In the opposite situation – no support at all – the word may well go round that it is not even worth asking. 'They don't want anyone to get qualified', buzzes the grapevine.

So, some consistency is desirable. Given the fact that most people want to encourage this sort of thing, a compromise needs to be found. The downside is that someone's absences are tolerated for a long while, costs are incurred – both from lost time and what that person could achieve, and from funding some aspect of the exercise – and then, proudly clutching their certificate, they amend their CV and head off into the distance. Equally, the positive side is a better-qualified employee who becomes more of an asset to the organisation.

It may be that the deal needs to be a little different at various levels or in different job functions. Certainly it should recognise the differences that exist among people: their age, job, responsibilities, length of service and, not least, the organisation's future intentions for them. But there should be a deal; and people should know what it is.

If sensible policy is discussed and decided, and if it is seen as resulting from some consultation and communication, and to reflect the interests of both parties, then there is no reason why staff should not see it as fair, reasonable – and helpful.

There may not simply be people who volunteer for this sort of thing. There may be others the organisation wants to actively encourage, or even insist, on going this route, so all the foregoing can be important.

a development continuum

It may be obvious, but warrants a brief word: a series of training activities may be regarded as just that – a series of disparate events. Or they may be linked, coordinated and move progressively and purposefully towards long-term objectives. The momentum and continuity of such an ongoing long-term process may allow the attainment of much more than a similar amount of time, and money, spent on more disparate things would do.

The merits of planning long term, or at least within a longer-term context, have been mentioned earlier. This thought is worth keeping in mind throughout this review.

secondment

For some companies a good, and convenient, way of developing people is to post them for short or long periods away from their present location. This may simply be to a branch office (or from a branch to HQ) or to a location where activity is specialised: a research facility perhaps.

For multinationals and others involved in business internationally, the tactic may typically involve overseas postings (or indeed job rotation). I was witness to this just recently when a relative of mine moved to the corporate headquarters of his (American) employer in the USA. This costs more than recruiting locally (he has four children to swell the costs!) but has a broader intention than just filling a post. Careers are not preordained, of course, but the thinking here is that all being well he will return (or go elsewhere in the organisation) having acquired experience to jump him up the corporate hierarchy faster than continuing to work in his home base would have done.

Some policy and guidelines for those seeking such opportunities may need to be laid down; similarly, HR departments will need a clear brief as to who is considered to go where, and how such decisions should be made. Some such may, of course, be part of ongoing development activity for individuals or functions.

There are various opportunities here, not all limited to large multinationals. For example, secondment may be arranged:

- in a different division of an organisation;
- in a subsidiary company;
- with a customer (or supplier) organisation;
- with the organisation of an agent or distributor;
- with a professional body (some of which are supported by their member companies seconding staff to them for a while; usually where there is reciprocal benefit).

It could be round the corner or thousands of miles away. You may well be able to think of, or use, other forms of secondment. Swaps – exchanges – are possible also, organised so that two people, and both organisational parties, benefit. This kind of arrangement might be essentially short term, say a week in the Paris office or, more relevant in this chapter, it might mean swapping roles and locations for a year or more.

sabbaticals

These may be regarded as something of a luxury. But a sabbatical can have real value, and be cost-effective too. It can take various forms, but in one company I worked with, one category of senior people was allowed to take six months (paid) leave after working with the company for 15 years. In consultancy – a fee-earning and time-dependent business – this had a real cost. Equally it was an organisation in which many did not habitually take long holidays because of the nature of the business, so in some ways the time was, in part, a quid pro quo.

Certainly it was highly motivational, both to those in the prescribed category and to those who aspired to be. I cannot now remember whether taking a sabbatical was compulsory, but such extended periods of leave often included a project, something to which no time would otherwise be given. For example, travel was one thing people sometimes wanted to do, and this linked usefully to the international development of the business, allowing more leisurely research and investigation than might otherwise have occurred. If this was coupled with some fee-earning work it made good sense all round.

There are a number of variables here, certainly:

- the duration selected;
- the number and level of staff to be involved;
- the purpose (or lack of it) given to the gap period;
- the reporting back, if appropriate.

One can think of all sorts of things this system could be used for, and one is certainly development. Part of the policy might be that if time were simply spent recharging the batteries, then although pay continued no other funding was given. An exception to this could be the choice of undertaking some mutually approved training or attending a training event.

individual motivation

Active careerists, a breed that becomes more numerous every moment given the dynamic times we live in, will want to take a long-term view and will act to take advantage of any aspect of their employee's attitude to, and provision for, development.

In a book directed towards managers' responsibilities for developing others, the main point of relevance here is one of perspective. Managers and their organisations have their own, maybe very specific, reasons for wanting to instigate development. But the need of the individual should be recognised; it will be nonetheless present for being ignored.

If the aims of the organisation and the needs of the individual can be made to coincide, this will strengthen the whole process. It has been said here, more than once, that development should be motivational. The most powerful motivational effect arises not as, or after, someone attends a training event – however much they enjoy it and find it useful. Rather it comes from their feeling that their personal long-term career aims are made easier to achieve by the way the organisation operates in the long term.

This kind of compatibility will keep good people with you, while you make them both better, more useful – and perhaps more likely to stay with you in the longer term.

monitoring progress

Given the time, effort and money that can go into development, there is clearly a need to make sure that what is done is worthwhile. Feedback is more than a reassurance of this: it provides an opportunity to fine-tune the activities and methods used. This may be simple, for example good feedback can produce a resolve to use a course or trainer again if the first experience is positive. Alternatively, it can be more complex in the sense that an in-company programme can be gradually adapted and improved to better reflect conditions as they change. Feedback can also assist with longer-term and sometimes organisation-wide developments such as the increasing use of computer- or Internet-based training.

Clearly there is also a prime need to see whether development activities bring changes in the people undertaking them. We want to know their reaction to them, and whether their knowledge, skills, attitudes and behaviour change.

There are various ways in which the results of development can be monitored. These are not mutually exclusive; you may usefully use a combination of different methods depending on circumstances. The intention should be twofold: first, to do the minimum that will produce the information needed, rather than allow an explosion of information to produce a glut of facts way beyond what is actually useful; second, to make the acquisition of the feedback straightforward. Systems, policy or people can sometimes have the reverse effect – there is the story of the hospital patient who had to telephone the hospital posing as a relative to discover how his state of health was viewed!

informal monitoring

Staff may sometimes complain that they never, or rarely, see their managers (others may, of course, complain they see them too much!). But if management time is skimped – no doubt because of other, seemingly more important pressures – then the first kind of contact to go will be ones linked to 'inessentials' such as development. After all, it is rationalised, operational matters must continue and be given priority.

The realities here can dilute the manager/staff relationship, inhibit motivation, and give rise to the sort of culture characterised by the remark, 'The only time I see my manager is if something has gone wrong'. So, time must be found for some meetings and for discussion about training matters. Further, this should be on a regular basis, rather than being the sort of thing that only occurs 'when time permits'. It should also be applied to all staff, rather than seeming to favour a few. While this may be necessary sometimes, one thing to avoid is spending most of your available time with any poor performers. While their situation may well need addressing, the greatest increase in performance can come from development activity applied to those already doing fine.

Informal monitoring can take many forms, for instance:

- meetings scheduled throughout the year to follow up annual appraisal sessions;
- fact-finding sessions to help plan future development activities;
- briefings about forthcoming training;
- debriefing after a course has been attended (or other training completed);
- counselling or monitoring of projects linked to training, either informal projects arranged between manager and staff or projects from sandwich courses (ie two course sessions linked with a project);
- items on the agenda of other (perhaps departmental) meetings addressing particular aspects of development;
- informal (and perhaps unstructured) meetings – as you pass on the stairs or chat over a sandwich.

There are more formal elements to some of these that link with comments under the headings that follow.

Two things will add power to this kind of activity. They are, first, a *continuing dialogue*, which implies the manager must make efforts to commit things to memory, or better still make a note, so that one exchange can be linked to the next, which will prove more effective than an ad hoc approach. Second, it is *always a two-way dialogue*: it will work better if people feel able to be involved, consulted and indeed feel that the whole process is something from which you intend them to gain.

The cumulative effect of this sort of activity should not be underestimated, nor should the impact of the simplest things. In my own case when I began writing – hesitatingly and inexpertly – for publication, my manager at that time took a real interest. His encouragement, comments and suggestions that I check this or think about that were instrumental in a major way in my acquiring sufficient skill to make writing a regular part of my work portfolio. Yet most of his inputs were often little more than remarks: 'Is there another way of putting that?', 'Could that be shorter?', 'Remember to keep it simple;

how many long words are there in that sentence?' Often they
were questions to which I had to supply the answer, though
advice was there as well – so were succinct ways of remem-
bering something. It was here, I think, in the interests of not
using long words unnecessarily that I first heard what is now
one of my favourite quotations, from Mark Twain, who said, 'I
never write the word "metropolis" if I get paid the same to
write the word "city".' From the management perspective the
continuity of this needs a little thought, but it needs no major
commitment of time or effort.

Forgive what may seem like a digression, but I believe my
situation described above helps make the point that the little
things are as important as the big; more so in some ways as
there is a more realistic prospect of finding opportunity and
time for them. Before long, doing so can become a habit for
any manager. In my case, more than 25 books later, I *know* just
how useful this kind of low-key input can be.

A final word to stress here is: *communication*. You will have
noticed that much that has been said about what needs to be
done in monitoring progress, indeed about getting the most
from development, is – in one way or another – communication. Although it cannot literally be true, a moral here is that
you cannot communicate too much about development.
Planning and managing to communicate sufficiently and in the
right way are crucial, and well worth striving towards. As we
move on, mention of communication will reoccur; no apology
for that.

testing training effectiveness

With certain kinds of training, measurement of its effectiveness
is fairly straightforward. This is very much the case when
training is directed primarily at imparting knowledge. You
want to know how much has 'stuck'. So, you can use a simple
test. This may be written or verbal, or involve one of several

computer technologies. For example a CD ROM can take users through a series of test questions, scoring and reinforcing knowledge in the event of error as they go.

Applications here range widely, but include matters such as product knowledge, numerical or procedural processes, keyboard or language skills and many more. Time spent here can be very useful. Knowing a test is coming may concentrate the mind of trainees and, at worst, it can pick up a complete lack of aptitude at an early stage before too much time and money are spent.

seeing for yourself

Sometimes the nature of the task, the development and the individual mean that there is a need both to observe and to get involved to correct anything necessary to improve or extend performance. A public manifestation of this is when we telephone a company and hear an announcement telling us that 'some calls may be recorded'. Sometimes, for example in the insurance industry, this is for legal reasons, but training is a prime reason too.

The essence of the activity here is that you observe something happening and then, if necessary, act on it either at once or later. This is not, however, just a question of negative critique (certainly not of threats) and demanding that things are done differently. Nor does it just describe the 'right way' and suggest people get on with it.

The process should be motivational – this is something that should be kept in mind throughout – and dealt with sensitively and systematically. This extends what has been said regarding on-the-job training, and there are classically five or six stages:

1. *Tell:* first make sure the individual knows exactly what to do. This is obviously doubly important if they or the

task are new. Make sure that your description of it is complete and unambiguous, and give every opportunity for them to ask questions (so do not say things like: 'I'm sure that's clear, it's easy enough. Any questions?', which will put them off asking).

2. *Show:* many tasks are best demonstrated. Sometimes what is being demonstrated is an exact methodology. Sometimes it is a general approach (for example, recording information in a customer database or writing a letter; the second will usually have elements that require the writer's judgement). It must be evident which is involved and the demonstration, like the instruction, must be clear and allow further exploration.

3. *Prompt practice:* once individuals are clear what to do then they can do it themselves. This might need to be under supervision initially, but once working alone then it is time for the next stage.

4. *Assess:* then the manager can assess how things are being done. How assessment is carried out will vary, but remember what was said earlier about ownership. A counselling approach that lets trainees assess themselves may be best, though equally the manager may need to make a more didactic input.

5. *Coach:* here the approach is as above. If change is necessary consider how best to achieve it and do not automatically just follow assessment with what amount to 'Do it this way' remarks. This, in effect, becomes the sort of input reviewed in Chapter 5.

6. *Agree follow up:* what needs to happen next will vary. It may be little or nothing. It could be that such a session forms the start (or is already a part of) an ongoing series of developmental inputs, or that something like a note in the diary, the individual's file or your own needs to be made. Knowing that the agreed follow-up will take place is very motivational for the

individual. Conversely, saying, 'Let's have brief word about that next week' and then forgetting is a waste – make notes.

The procedure described in this section will need to be considered in the light of the experience of the trainee. The principles described apply to first-time briefing and, with a less 'from scratch' approach, to tasks which have to be regularly checked.

A final comment here concerns the place where this sort of session is conducted. It may be informal, straightforward and cause no problem to conduct it at the trainee's desk, even if the workstation is in an open-plan area. Or it might be better if such a session were more private. Additionally, some jobs and tasks do not take place in the workplace and yet still have to be observed and worked on in this kind of way. A classic example of this is the field sales job. Sales managers should regularly accompany members of their sales team, sitting in on meetings for evaluation purposes and discussing them later – at what is, in sales, called a 'kerbside conference' because it often takes place in the salesperson's car. Sometimes the nature of the sales process means that this observation can even be done without the customer's knowledge, as in publishing where many retail calls are conducted out in a bookshop and a manager can browse nearby and listen.

Judgement is needed regarding place, as a trainee feeling awkward (because his or her colleagues can hear, for instance) will be less likely to concentrate, while a manager constantly interrupted by other things will find the same.

course assessment

Here we look at the measurement associated with training courses of whatever sort: these include attendance on public programmes, courses held in-house (and conducted either by internal staff or an outside trainer), even the use of training packages.

Sometimes courses may be used for motivational or other reasons; most often we want to know that they have met their objectives and are likely to have some positive effect on action. Measurement may take a little time, though not an unreasonable amount and only a small percentage of the actual training time. It can involve several stages, some of which might be omitted or dealt with more simply; however any decisions to do that should be made carefully. So, consider:

■ *A pre-course briefing.* This may include a discussion about the choice of course (or the choice to do some training), and should ensure that both manager and trainee are agreed on why attendance is desirable and what should be got from it. It may take an overall view or go into some detail, for example creating a checklist of points that should be raised on the course (as a trainer I like nothing better than when people attend courses with a clear idea of how they hope to benefit).

■ *An evaluation form.* At most courses an evaluation form will be used. This may be for the benefit of the trainer or organiser, and an organisation may have its own form, designed to its requirements and issued to those attending public seminars. These are useful in providing an immediate impression of the course, its content and form, and a copy may be usefully retained. An example is shown in Figure 8.1. The form shown is used by the Institute of Management, among whose faculty of trainers I am included (they offer both public and in-house training and can be contacted at the address shown in the figure). Another similar form worth a look is that used by what many know as the National Training Index, now part of the organisation Thinq Limited. It is an independent body providing an excellent means of assessing externally available training, along with training packages and venues. It may be worth checking out; you can contact them, tel: 020 7871 4007.

▨ *A post-course debriefing*. The fact that a form exists should not blind you to the merits of sitting down with someone on their return from training. Such a session is best planned, and even scheduled, before attendance takes place. The completed form may act as an agenda or checklist for a discussion and the onus then is likely to be on the future – for example, what action or further training will follow. Sometimes further documentation may be useful, perhaps to put something on file as a guide to future users of the same programme.

▨ *Longer-term review*. It may also be worth considering a longer-term review. This is because, first, many courses seem good in the immediate aftermath: it was interesting, fun and a few days away from the office – but what matters most is the way behaviour is changed in the future. Second, such a review can link to specific projects and to the actual job. For example, people attending a report-writing course may be asked to write a report for discussion with their manager or, better still, use the next one they have to write as a basis of discussion designed to extend the thinking started on the training, and consider how useful it has been. Such longer-term reviews may involve meetings and further evaluation forms or reports.

▨ *The link to appraisal*. Ultimately individual training inputs may come up for discussion at the next formal job appraisal. As has been mentioned elsewhere, development is a prime consideration in such sessions.

Not least, the whole sequence described here bestows importance on training as a process, and on the individual development taking place. It is thus motivational for the individual concerned, as well as providing feedback and a basis for action for both manager and staff. Incidentally, it is worth noting that your staff have probably come across the advice that this should be done. They may well expect it, and think less well of an employer who does not do it.

annual job appraisal

As this has been commented on earlier in the review, no great detail is required here. Suffice to say that this is the annual culmination of all the checks and discussions held during the year. It provides an opportunity to review the net result of all training and development undertaken during the year, is a good moment to comment on the most recent activity and, of course, to discuss the continuation of what is usually an ongoing process.

the ultimate alternative

Whatever training and development occur, and whatever monitoring of results follows, there is no absolute certainty that it will work. Occasionally it becomes clear that an individual will never make the grade. This may be for all sorts of reasons: poor selection, lack of motivation, sheer inability – whatever. Sometimes the reason provides useful feedback; for example, poor selection might hold a moral for future recruitment which, handled differently, might produce better candidates. On other occasions it is simply a fact of life – not everyone can do everything. It may also be a side-effect of technology, with someone moved from, say, a bank branch customer service role to one of the call centres that now substitute for much of that activity, finding they cannot cope with the computer systems involved.

the Institute
of Management

COURSE ASSESSMENT

OPEN PROGRAMMES

Please complete this form before you leave, as this will help our future planning. As we are also interested in the long-term value of our training programmes we shall contact a sample of participants by telephone after the course to ask for their comments. I would like to thank you in advance for your help.

Pippa Bourne

Course Title.. Date.................................

Name .... Job Title ....

Organisation ....

Training Manager's Name.. Telephone number ....

Please circle the appropriate response.	Comment *(Please comment on your response rating)*
1. What is your overall opinion of the course? 1 2 3 4 5 6 very good very poor	
2. How would you rate the Course Leader's presentation? 1 2 3 4 5 6 very good very poor	
3. In your opinion, did the course meet the objectives set out in the course brochure? 1 2 3 4 5 6 very well very poorly	
4. What is your opinion of the course materials? *(Course papers, visual aids etc)* 1 2 3 4 5 6 very good very poor	
5. What was your opinion of the venue? 1 2 3 4 5 6 very good very poor	
6. How well was your booking/enquiry dealt with? 1 2 3 4 5 6 very well very poorly	

Figure 8.1   *Institute of Management evaluation form*

7. Was the level of content? *(Please tick appropriate box)*

Much too advanced ☐   Too advanced ☐   Just right ☐   Too basic ☐   Much too basic ☐

8. Do you feel the course can be improved by the inclusion or expansion of certain topics? *(If so, which?)*

9. In your opinion would the course work better without certain topics? *(If so, which?)*

10. Has the course provided you with any ideas or actions which could be implemented at work?

11. Was sufficient time allowed to answer your questions and discuss your particular issues?   Yes ☐ / No ☐

12. Would you recommend the course to a colleague?   Yes ☐ / No ☐

13. If the answer to the above question was 'no', why not?

14. Was it your idea to attend the course?   Yes ☐ / No ☐

15. If not, who brought it to your attention (name and job title please)?

16. Were you given a copy of our short course brochure to see the course content?   Yes ☐ / No ☐

17. What other course subjects are of interest to you?

18. How did your organisation hear about the course?

IM Brochure	*(Please state how obtained)*	....
Advertisement	*(Please state which)*	....
Within own organisation	*(Please give details)*	....
Other source	*(Please give details)*	....

☐ If you are interested in running this course tailored to your organisation's requirements, please tick this box and we will contact you.

Please hand the completed form in at reception.

Mrs Jean Morton
The Institute of Management
Management House
Cottingham Road
Corby
Northants NN17 1TT

Figure 8.1 *Institute of Management evaluation form (continued)*

Given poor – unacceptable – performance, the choices are few. You can:

■ Put up with it (which is not to be recommended).
■ Apply some sort of remedial action (classically, development or training, though it might be that motivation needs boosting).
■ Change procedures (maybe what is being asked is unreasonable, few could perform acceptably and only new approaches or methods will ensure the required performance).
■ Terminate the employment of the person concerned.

The rules here are simple. Having checked things like procedures and motivation, development must be provided if the problem is a skill shortfall of some sort. If appropriate – even sustained – development is given a fair chance and performance is still not improving, then the only option may be to fire someone. This is not something to be done lightly, and is unpleasant for you, the employee and those around you. But when push comes to shove it may have to be done. No one likes it if a team carries passengers, least of all when others must make up the shortfall. Ultimately your job is to produce results and problems of underperformance must be tackled.

Few, arguably no, things that are difficult become easier if delayed. It is all too easy, given the way it is usually viewed, to put off this sort of ultimate action, rationalising and waiting for improvement that, in all honesty, is not actually on the cards. Once the point has been reached where the reason for poor performance is clearly established, and the alternatives have been explored and exhausted, then swift action is usually best. This can be tempered with a benevolent policy about severance arrangements, and this is something many organisations favour for motivational and public relations reasons. Remember, too, the legal aspects of this situation.

onwards and upwards

While it is necessary to include the previous section, it does not suggest that training cannot more usually cure the problems that occur. Indeed performance potential may provide opportunities for people to progress far beyond their original post or even their intention, and for the organisation to benefit from their career progress.

So, on a positive note, it is to this we move in the final chapter.

career implications

In this last chapter we look further ahead. Development must be justified and very often this means that it must produce results in the short term. This is fair enough; indeed training may be instigated specifically to produce a prompt effect. On the other hand development may have longer-term objectives, and will certainly have – wittingly or otherwise – longer-term results.

Two prime aspects of the long-term link between development and careers are, first, the manager's responsibility to 'grow talent' and ensure succession, to develop those who will inhabit key positions in the organisation in future with an eye on their promotion (and in so doing to assist appropriate and desired staff retention); second, the individual's need for career success, whether within their current organisation or beyond. Career progression is something that individuals will, if they are sensible, pursue in any case – helping the process will usually prove motivational.

In order to fit development to career planning, it is necessary to keep in mind the scope of what this now involves for many people. Why, in fact, is career planning necessary?

the need to plan careers

Business pundits and economists predict a range of varying scenarios for the future of the work environment. But one thing we can all agree about – it will be uncertain. We live in dynamic times. The old world of job security, jobs for life, prescribed ladders of promotion and gradually increasing success and rewards has gone, replaced by talk of downsizing (and 'right-sizing' makes it sound no better), redundancy, short-term contracts, teleworking, and portfolio careers.

Waiting for things to 'get back to normal' is simply not one of the options. No one can guarantee him- or herself a successful career, but it is something that everyone can influence to some degree. Indeed it is something that most surely *want* to influence. We all spend a great deal of time at work. It is important to make sure that time is as enjoyable and rewarding as possible. There is a line in one of John Lennon's songs: 'Life is what happens while you are making other plans.' It encapsulates a painful thought. There is perhaps no worse situation to get into than one where we look back and say to ourselves: 'If only...'.

So, with no rigid, preordained career ladder to follow, careers need planning. The question is how to do it. The bad news is that there is no magic formula. Sorry, but just snapping your fingers and shouting 'Promotion!' will not make you Chief Executive overnight (if you *can* do this please let me know how!). You can, however, make a positive difference if you work at it. The starting point is that people must know what they want, and this needs some systematic self-analysis.

setting a course

Consider this from the point of view of your own career and remember that the situation for others is similar. There are several stages of thinking that are useful:

▨ Assess your skills: you may be surprised how many you have in, for example:
  - communications;
  - influencing;
  - managing (people or projects);
  - problem solving;
  - creativity;
  - social skills;
  - numeracy;
  - special skills (everything from languages to computer usage).

▨ Assess you work values: here you should consider factors such as:
  - a strong need to achieve;
  - a need for a high salary;
  - a liking for doing something 'worthwhile';
  - a desire to be creative;
  - other factors, from travel to being independent or working as part of a team.

▨ Assess your personal characteristics: you are a risk taker, an innovator, or someone who can work under pressure? Consider what kind of person you are and how these characteristics affect your work situation.

▨ Assess your non-work characteristics: factors such as family commitments, where you want to live and how much time you are happy to spend away from home.

▨ Match your analysis to the market demands: in other words consider how well your overall capabilities and characteristics fit the market opportunities. This avoids you seeking out a route that is doomed before it starts. If anything to do with computers, say, throws you, then you either have to learn (and these days learn fast) or avoid areas of work dependent on a high degree of computer literacy.

With all this in mind you can set clear objectives; the old adage that if you do not know where you are going any road will do, is nowhere more true. Aim high. You can always trade down, but you may be more successful than you think and it is a pity to miss something not because it is unachievable, but only because you do not try for it.

From here on the management of your career progress is in the details, and the first step is to realise just that.

perception is reality

Of course, progress is dependent, probably to a major degree, on performance. Unless you deliver, you will have little chance of being judged able to cope with greater or different responsibility, and promotion may – rightly – allude you. But other things have an effect too.

Consider an example. Someone is asked to manage a project, something like moving the office to a new location. It is important. There is a great deal hanging on it and it is multifaceted. The person may have all the necessary characteristics. They can do the necessary groundwork, they are thorough and forget nothing. They balance all the various – probably conflicting – criteria and document a sound recommendation and plan. So far so good – then they are asked to present it to the Board.

Making a formal presentation is not everyone's stock in trade. Some are nervous, they do not know how to prepare, to put it over well, or stick to the time given to them and it proves, to say the least, somewhat lacklustre. What happens? Do people say, 'Never mind, it was a sound plan'? They are much more likely to take the view that the ideas themselves are suspect; perhaps they act accordingly and put the whole thing on hold or take some other action. And what happens next time such a project needs allocating? The person concerned is not even in the running. We have touched on this sort of thing

before. The skills shortfall can leave ;
tion stillborn. Beyond that, here it i:
career progress that is of concern.

This example makes an importan
allied experience too) are rightly re
other words, they are not simply im
they are especially important to how people are seen and
they get on.

active career management

There is a long list of skills that should be regarded in this way. In many management jobs they include all aspects of managing people, presentation and business writing, numeracy and often, these days, IT skills. Many such factors are to do with aspects of communication. In addition, there are more general skills such as good time management. Productivity is as important as results. Another characteristic of modern organisational life is that everyone seems to have more and more to do. Some people cope with this better than others. They are better organised; they recognise the 80/20 rule – that a comparatively small amount of activity will give rise to a large proportion of the desired outputs. Not only is their life a little less hectic or pressured, they are able to achieve more; and it shows.

Thus one area of active career management consists of recognising what career skills can help you and making sure that you excel in them.

In addition, there are a host of other factors that have an influence on how you progress. Who you know is often cited as being as important as what you know. Some people seem very well connected. But this does not just happen. They probably work at it: they note their contacts, they seek out new ones, they keep in touch and recognise that this is a two-way process. And it helps.

ay ahead

ve careerists do not rely on good luck (this is more likely to
the reason your 'competitors' in the organisation are
successful!). They do, however, take advantage of any good
fortune that comes their way. And their planning and positive
attitude to the process makes it more likely that they can do so.

What is necessary is an all-embracing approach to what is
essentially a lifelong campaign. Those who leave no stone
unturned, who look at every detail of their work life in terms of
its career implications, tend to do best. If they have thought
through what they want to do and if they have clear objectives,
then – while they may not achieve everything they want – they
will get closer to their ideal. This is true whether you seek to
make progress within one large organisation, or whether you
realistically see your career changing several times as the years
go by.

For the most part, careers do not just happen, they are made.
You can do worse than start a more active phase of career
development by recognising this and seeing your career as
likely to be made primarily – by you.

the management response

There may well be personal lessons here, but let us return the
focus to the manager's responsibility for his or her team. What
are the implications of this? There are several; managers must:

■ *Recognise the concern and intentions of individuals:*
the factors reviewed above are real, indeed are
growing in importance, and will influence people's
thinking and actions. For example, requests may be
made for training that may seem of little relevance in
the short term, but are explained by career intentions.

▓ *Incorporate longer-term intentions in development plans:* sometimes these are primarily motivated by organisational factors such as promotion and new future jobs, but you also need to keep an eye on what people will see as individually beneficial in a career sense.

▓ *Link development to appraisal:* ensure that discussions about development (what is necessary, what is planned and has been done) touch on longer-term issues as well as focusing on next year's required performance.

▓ *Communicate:* tell people often and in sufficient detail how development will help them in the short and long term – of course people need to know the organisational reasons for any training, but the effect on the individual must not be neglected.

▓ *Specifically set long-term 'career' objectives where appropriate:* these may apply to such matters as planned succession, or to people generally regarded as high flyers (but for whom no target slot is yet identified).

Sometimes career implications are, at least to start with, unstated. They are simply in the mind of the manager. On other occasions they are made clear to individuals, or more widely – with some organisations having so-called 'fast track' routes, designed to provide accelerated development and experience of a wide range of corporate activities.

Remember the priority hope of so many members of staff – 'I want to work for a manager from whom I learn.' The reasons are clear; they link to job satisfaction, but also to career progress. Helping people to grow benefits you and the organisation in the short term. It may help in the long term also – as things change, new opportunities open up and new recruits are sought internally to move into positions that will expand success. If, ultimately, some people do leave then so be it. You will have had good value from them during their tenure with you, you may have increased that value by extending that tenure somewhat and, as has been said, no one ever leaving is actually a negative option, one that would ultimately promote only mediocrity.

Thus development and careers are integrally bound up. You cannot have development activity in play *without* affecting the career aspects of those involved. The implications of considering career and job alongside each other one that developmental thinking, plans and implementation are stronger. It is one of the ways by which development can be made effective, and in which its motivational effect can also be enhanced.

afterword

When you're through changing, you're through.
Change is a process, not a goal; a journey, not
a destination.

Robert Kriegal and David Brant

The world of work is likely to remain competitive and volatile, and change is the one certainty we all face. To succeed – to achieve the results with which we are charged – all those in the world of work must be firing on all cylinders. There is no room for half measures; and there are so often no second prizes. To succeed in this dynamic environment, managers must be in a position to rely on the consistent good performance of their staff.

Thus a manager's job is to ensure that people can (and want) to do the right thing. There may be a great deal hanging on their actions and the standard to which they operate. Any managers who skimp their development responsibilities risk giving themselves and their department or organisation a serious handicap. This may act, day by day, to dilute the efficiency and effectiveness of operations and, at worst, may end as the cause of failure to produce the planned results.

By imparting knowledge, developing skills and changing attitudes, successful training and development can:

- ▓ act as a significant motivator (and have a positive impact on factors such as staff retention);
- ▓ change and improve performance short term;
- ▓ ensure long-term operational excellence is maintained;
- ▓ keep people and organisations ahead of change, externally and internally;
- ▓ create differentiation in the marketplace through the way people interact externally.

There is, as with so much in management, no magic formula to guarantee instant success. It needs a systematic approach, it needs planning and it needs care in execution. It can – and must – utilise an increasingly wide and disparate range of development methods. The simplest action may, in either the short or long term, be as useful and as significant in its results as something more complex.

If there is anything that comes near to a magic formula, or which at least offers a clue to how to proceed overall, it is *continuity*. The way ahead is to maintain a continuing focus on development. This involves:

- ▓ planning ahead and anticipating events (as far as possible);
- ▓ reacting accurately when surprises occur (as they will);
- ▓ taking action progressively, whether what is done is major or minor;
- ▓ letting the cumulative effect of different things build up;
- ▓ adopting a broad view of the people and the organisation.

In this way, the positive effect of development gradually builds. It will then add power to operations and give satisfaction to those who participate in it. It is a process that never ends. The attitude that 'even the best performance can be improved' is a sound one; or as John Wooden put it - 'It's what you learn after you know it all that counts.' And ultimately the time and effort any developmental activity takes will be reflected in the ongoing results that people are able to achieve.

Your people may, rightly, be given the credit for what *they* achieve; *you* may take credit for the fact that you have helped put them in a position where they deserve it.

postscript: a warning

A number of matters touched on in this book, such as recruitment, appraisal, terms and contracts of employment and more, are affected by employment legislation.

This is something that, in the UK at least, is complex and ever-changing. Mention of the laws concerned with discrimination of various sorts is sufficient to make the point. Much here is, of course, not controversial. The law specifies things most of us would want to do anyway to be fair to both individuals and organisation alike.

However, in an increasingly litigious age, ensuring that everything is done – and recorded – correctly is important. Transgressions can cause major problems, as anyone who has spent lengthy hours in an industrial tribunal will testify.

This is mentioned here only as a reminder: the full implications of employment legislation are beyond the scope of this publication. If you feel you need advice in this area, check; ignorance or wrong assumptions could prove expensive.

other titles in the Kogan Page creating success series

Be Positive by Phil Clements
Business Etiquette by David Robinson
Develop Your Assertiveness by Sue Bishop
Develop Your NLP Skills by Andrew Bradbury
E-Business Essentials by Matt Haig
Empowering People by Jane Smith
How to Beat Your Competitors by John G Fisher
How to Generate Great Ideas by Barrie Hawkins
How to Manage Organisational Change by D E Hussey
How to Motivate People by Patrick Forsyth
How to Run a Successful Conference by John G Fisher
How to Write a Marketing Plan by John Westwood
Improve Your Communication Skills by Alan Barker
Improving Employee Performance by Nigel Harrison
Make Every Minute Count by Marion E Hayes
Make That Call! by Iain Maitland
Making Innovation Happen by Michael Morgan
Organise Yourself by John Caunt
Performance Appraisals by Bob Havard
Stay Confident by John Caunt
Successful Presentation Skills by Andrew Bradbury
Successful Project Management by Trevor Young
Team Building by Robert B Maddux
Using the Internet Faster and Smarter by Brooke Broadbent
Write That Letter! by Iain Maitland
Writing Effective E-mail by Nancy Flynn and Tom Flynn

forthcoming titles

Communication at Work by Judith Taylor
How to Write a Business Plan by Brian Finch
Taking Minutes of Meetings by Joanna Gutmann